Einfühlung

Reclaiming the Radical Power of Empathy in
Leadership, Work, and a World That's Lost Its Feel

David S. Morgan

Prologue
THE CIRCLE THAT CHANGED ME

It was November 2003, and the air on Whidbey Island carried the sharp stillness of early winter. I had come from the world of product development and innovation: roadmaps, whiteboards, prototypes. Design thinking was our compass, and empathy was its foundation. I believed in it. Practiced it. Taught it.

But here I was, standing in a timber-framed retreat center just off the coast of Seattle, surrounded by a circle of strangers from around the world: peacemakers, diplomats, facilitators, artists, and activists. People who had come not to solve, but to listen.

The gathering was called The Practice of Peace, and it was rooted in Open Space Technology. There was no agenda. No keynote. Just an invitation, simple and spacious: "What do you care about? What are you willing to host?"

As we sat in that open room, something unexpected happened. People rose. Ideas surfaced. Conversations formed like eddies in a stream. I watched as participants leaned in with urgency and tenderness, speaking truths that rarely had a home. Former adversaries shared stories. Skeptics became stewards. Conflict gave way to collaboration, not because of structure, but because of space.

And I felt it: something shift inside me.

It wasn't the cleverness of the method that stayed with me. It was the quality of presence in that room. The way people listened. The way silence held weight. The way the room itself became a kind of nervous system, registering what mattered, what hurt, what longed to be named.

We weren't just exchanging ideas. We were sensing something together.

For the first time, I glimpsed empathy not as a mindset or method but as a living system. A shared field. A generative force that could move through people, processes, and places if we knew how to listen for it.

It wasn't performative. It wasn't strategic. It was presence that moved between us.

Later, I would learn the word that gave me language for what I experienced: *Einfühlung*. "Feeling into" another's experience, another's truth, another's world. Not from a distance, but from within.

That moment didn't replace what I had known about innovation. It deepened it. It reshaped how I led teams, how I convened stakeholders, how I held space for ambiguity. It taught me that empathy wasn't just something we practice in user interviews—it's something we design for, not as a step in a process, but as the atmosphere that allows emergence.

From that day forward, I began to lead differently: with structure and space, with answers and presence, with empathy not just for the end user but for the system itself.

On the final day of the gathering, we convened once more in silence. A closing circle. A talking stick. One by one, people rose, walked to the center of the room, and spoke from the heart:

"I am an activist. I live in Israel." "I am a teacher. I come from Rwanda." "I am a mother, a survivor, a seeker..."

And then the stick reached me.

I stood, walked to the center, and suddenly... I couldn't reduce myself to a role, a label, or a biography. The words felt too small. The categories, too brittle.

So I said simply, "I am."

I held the moment—still, uncertain, alive—for what felt like forever.

Then I sat back down.

That moment has stayed with me ever since. Not because I said something profound, but because I felt something real. In that room, held by strangers and story and silence, I remembered what it meant to simply be.

This book is born from that remembering. But it is not a book about empathy as we've come to know it.

Empathy today has been flattened into technique. We've made it performative: the right words, measured tones, strategic nods. But presence is not performance.

This book reclaims empathy's deeper roots in *Einfühlung*—not analyzing from a distance, but sensing from within. It's about empathy as a living system rather than leadership skill. It's about empathy as infrastructure: the embodied capacity to sense and respond within complex systems.

What I discovered in that circle on Whidbey Island became the foundation for everything that follows. The book unfolds in three parts, each emerging from what that room taught me:

Part I: What We Forgot explores how empathy became performance and what we lost in translation. We'll examine empathy not as individual capacity but as collective infrastructure—the nervous system that allows groups, teams, and organizations to sense and respond together.

Part II: The Human Engine Cycle reveals five expressions of empathy in motion: Feel, Discern, Imagine, Respond, Replenish. These aren't steps to follow. but rhythms to recognize—the natural flow I witnessed as that room breathed with collective awareness.

Part III: Scaling the Sacred examines how empathic sensing moves through leadership and organizations without losing its essence. How do we design for the kind of presence that transforms not just individuals but entire systems?

This book doesn't end with certainty. It ends with motion.

If you've ever felt too much in a culture that rewards numbness, if you've ever led from intuition in a world that preferred strategy, if you've wondered whether there's a way to connect without leaving yourself behind—you belong here.

Like that talking stick circle, this is an invitation into presence. Into the space between knowing and being. Into empathy not as performance, but as the living system that connects us all.

TABLE OF CONTENTS

INTRODUCTION

The Ache We Ignore in a World That's Lost Its Feel

There's something we rarely say aloud, especially not in boardrooms or design labs. But we feel it. Even when the metrics look strong. Even when the strategy aligns. Even when the team performs. We feel the thinning.

A quiet unraveling of meaning. A dulling of aliveness. A widening gap between what we perform and what we are.

Last week, a CEO told me, "We hit every target. Stock price is up 40%. And I've never felt more empty."

This isn't burnout. It's not failure. Not crisis. It's something older, deeper—an ache that sits just beneath the surface.

The ache of being human in a world that rewards us for forgetting.

The Great Acceleration

We build faster. We optimize harder. We lead with grit, vision, and dashboards. But in the rush to scale and prove, something essential slips away.

We feel it in our bodies—that tension between shoulder blades that never fully releases. We hear it in the silence between meetings, the pause where meaning used to live. We see it in our teams, the brightness dimming behind the performance.

We've engineered our way into numbness at the moment we most need to feel.

The evidence isn't just anecdotal. In 2023, Gallup reported that only 23% of employees worldwide feel engaged at work—the lowest in a decade. Leadership turnover has reached crisis levels. Employee wellbeing metrics have plummeted, even as wellness perks multiply.

And beneath the statistics: Wells Fargo's phantom accounts. Boeing's deadly shortcuts. Theranos's elaborate deception.

Each began the same way: smart people stopped feeling the signals their bodies knew.

This disconnection isn't just personal. It's systemic.

The Real Conditions of Leadership

We are leading in an era of relentless disruption. Not just fast change—compound, cross-cutting pressure.

The average lifespan of an S&P 500 company has decreased from approximately 61 years to 16 (Innosight, 2017; McKinsey & Company, 2023). Artificial intelligence capabilities are advancing rapidly, with significant improvements in performance occurring on a scale of months, while governance frameworks struggle to adapt, often hindered by regulatory and organizational delays (McKinsey & Company, 2023; PwC, 2024).

And leaders? We're asked to navigate all this while delivering quarterly results, preserving culture, and staying sane.

The problem isn't that we're unprepared. It's that we've been trained to override the very intelligence we need most.

We've lost the capacity to feel.

And when we stop feeling, we stop adapting.

Beyond the Empathy We've Been Sold

This book is not a defense of empathy as we have come to know it—the soft skills training, the emotional intelligence frameworks, the performed concern that leaves everyone feeling more isolated than before.

This is a reclamation of something deeper. Something that was lost when we translated the German *Einfühlung* into our sanitized version of empathy. Something that knows the difference between connection and performance, between presence and politeness.

What we've called empathy was never meant to be comfortable. It was meant to be alive.

This book argues that empathy is not a trait to possess but a capacity to activate. Not sentiment, but structure. Not soft, but systemic. And it offers a framework for putting this understanding into practice: what we call The Human Engine.

The Human Engine

To meet the moment we're in, we don't just need better strategies or smarter systems. We need a return to our full human capacity, not as performance, not as sentiment, but as infrastructure.

The Human Engine is a regenerative cycle of five interwoven capacities that keep people, teams, and systems alive. These aren't competencies to master, but design principles to embed and ways of working that remain human even under pressure.

When these capacities flow together, they create something our organizations desperately need: the ability to sense what systems cannot yet say, to choose wisely when values collide, to dream beyond what seems practical, to act with integrity when pressure mounts, and to renew where burnout has been normalized.

This is not a book of best practices. It's a guide to living ones.

An Urgent Reclamation

This reclamation has never been more urgent. As AI systems claim to replicate "empathy" through pattern recognition, the need to distinguish genuine human connection from its simulation grows more critical. The future of work, leadership, and possibly humanity itself depends on reclaiming what algorithms cannot replicate: the embodied wisdom of feeling into complexity with presence, discernment, and moral imagination.

An Invitation

This book is for the ones who feel too much. Who sense what's broken even when no one names it. Who carry a quiet hope that work can still be human.

If you're the executive tired of shallow transformation, the product leader who hears what the metrics miss, the founder whose vision has outgrown conventional tools, the changemaker who still believes meaning is not optional—welcome.

The journey ahead is not a blueprint. It's a reawakening.

We begin not with answers, but with sensation. Not with control, but with connection. Not with confidence, but with courage.

The organizations that shape the future won't be the most efficient or most profitable. They'll be the most alive.

The ones that can feel.

Feeling is not our weakness. It's our edge.

PART I

WHAT WE FORGOT

Empathy was never meant to be comfortable. It was meant to be alive.

Before empathy became a buzzword, flattened into technique and stripped of discomfort, it was *Einfühlung*: the radical act of feeling into another's world while remaining rooted in your own.

This part is a remembering.

If something in you knows there's more to empathy than performance, you're right.

This is not where the journey ends. It's where it begins: with the ache, the signal, the remembering.

Empathy in Motion
The Human Engine Cycle: Five Capacities for
Adaptive Embodied Leadership

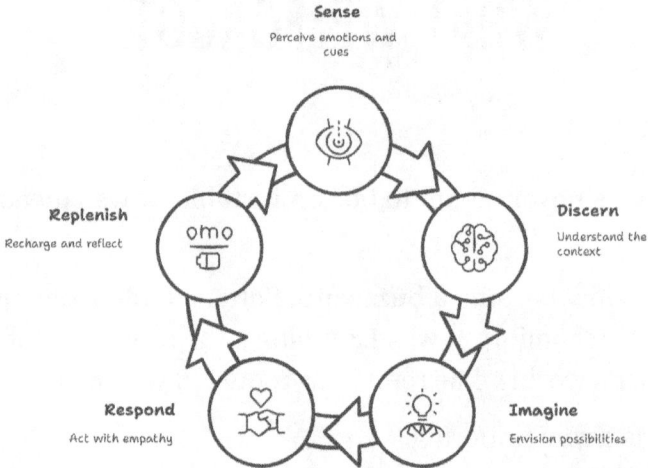

Sense
Perceive emotions and
cues

Replenish
Recharge and reflect

Discern
Understand the
context

Respond
Act with empathy

Imagine
Envision possibilities

Empathy in Motion: The Human Engine Cycle

The Five Capacities Adaptive Embodied Leadership

Empathy isn't a trait we possess—it's a cycle we practice. These five capacities—Sense, Discern, Imagine, Respond, and Replenish—form a continuous rhythm of awareness, insight, creativity, action, and renewal. Together, they power an adaptive, human-centered way of leading, creating, and connecting in complexity.

Chapter I

THE EMPATHY WE FORGOT

Reclaiming the Radical Power of *Einfühlung*

"Empathy is the willingness to be disturbed."
— **Margaret J. Wheatley**

Empathy has been reduced to technique—and it often fails us as a result.

She raised her hand, then let it fall. The manager had already moved on, talking over her as if she weren't there. She knew better than to ask again.

The boy stood motionless in the hallway, hands pressed to his ears. No one stopped. Not because they didn't care, but because they didn't see. We call it policy. We call it protocol. But what we've built is a machine of disconnection.

Disconnection is not a symptom. It is the system.

This reveals a troubling pattern: our systems aren't failing because they're broken. They're failing because they're executing a design that rewards detachment and suppresses empathy.

The teacher sees defiance where there's sensory overload. The manager hears attitude where there's exhaustion. The system demands compliance where humanity asks for understanding.

In many dominant Western institutions (schools, hospitals, corporations) we've designed disconnection in. Not as cruelty, but as efficiency. Not as malice, but as muscle memory. We designed it out of systems to reduce friction, eliminate ambiguity, and protect those in power from discomfort. In doing so, we streamlined away the signals that would've helped us adapt.

Sociologist Arlie Hochschild's research reveals how organizations systematically commodify caring through "emotional labor": requiring workers to perform emotions they may not feel while suppressing authentic responses (Hochschild, 1983). Flight attendants smile through harassment, healthcare workers provide comfort while being measured only on efficiency, customer service representatives absorb anger without support for processing the emotional residue. This creates empathy fatigue not because caring depletes us, but because we do it without systemic support.

This chapter is a reckoning with what empathy has become in modern leadership, and a reclamation of what it could be.

1.1 The Performance Problem

Marcus watched his team leader carefully compose "the empathy expression." Eyes softening at the corners, head tilted slightly, brow furrowed just enough to signal concern without suggesting actual distress.

"I hear what you're saying," she said, voice modulated to the precise tone of corporate care, "and I really understand how difficult this reorganization has been for everyone."

Marcus nodded, noticing the familiar hollowness spreading in his chest. The words were technically perfect—they'd all been through

4

the same leadership training—but they landed like stones in still water, creating ripples without depth.

He noticed his colleagues exchanging glances. They'd prepared for this conversation for weeks, gathering courage to bring forward their concerns about burnout, impossible timelines, and the toll the latest restructuring was taking on their mental health.

"I feel your frustration," she continued, nodding to acknowledge each person around the table before glancing at her watch. "Now, let's pivot to solutions. I've got another meeting in ten minutes, but I want each of you to know my door is always open."

The phrase hung in the air, a promise everyone recognized as performative. Her door—like her attention—was rarely open outside these scheduled moments of "connection."

What was meant to signal empathy instead confirmed its absence, leaving the team feeling more isolated than before they'd gathered their courage to speak.

The Performance Trap

This scene plays out daily across organizations worldwide. Leaders trained in the outward signals of empathy without the inward practice of presence. Teams hungry for genuine connection settling for choreographed concern.

Today's leadership landscape is littered with these performances. We maintain eye contact, mirror body language, and generate the right facial expressions. We say "I understand" with practiced sincerity. We deploy validation phrases and active listening techniques with mechanical precision.

These aren't inherently bad skills, but they are, at best, the scaffolding upon which genuine empathic encounter might be built. At worst, they are sophisticated mimicry, allowing us to appear empathic without risking actual connection (Hojat et al., 2011).

Genuine empathy is not a technique. It is an encounter.

But performance is only part of the problem. Even when our empathy is sincere, it is not always fair, or effective. Critics like psychologist Paul Bloom have shown that empathy is biased, parochial, and prone to causing distress rather than action (Bloom, 2016). A CEO tears up hearing about her VP's child's cancer diagnosis, immediately offering flexible work arrangements. That same morning, she denied sick leave to a warehouse worker whose mother is dying, the request buried in HR paperwork she'll never see.

This isn't cruelty. It's architecture. Our empathy flows through the channels proximity creates.

Bloom's critique has merit: unchecked empathy can indeed be discriminatory and ineffective. Yet, his solution—rational compassion—risks repeating the same detachment that caused the crisis. Research by psychologist C. Daniel Batson demonstrates that empathy, when guided by ethical frameworks, consistently motivates altruistic behavior even across group differences (Batson, 2011). The answer isn't to abandon empathy but to mature it—integrating emotional resonance with discernment, presence with principle.

Even when empathy does activate, it doesn't always lead to constructive action. Neuroscientists distinguish between empathic distress and compassionate response (Singer & Klimecki, 2014). Empathic distress occurs when witnessing another's suffering triggers overwhelming personal discomfort. Rather than motivating prosocial action, this distress often leads to avoidance, withdrawal, or burnout.

What we suppress becomes systemic.

So what do we do when empathy as sentiment fails us, and empathy as technique falls flat? We begin again, not with performance, but with motion. And not with modern empathy, but with its deeper root.

1.2 What We Forgot to Remember

Before empathy became a buzzword, flattened into technique and stripped of discomfort, it was Einfühlung: the radical act of feeling into another's world while remaining rooted in your own.

The Forgotten Lineage

Einfühlung wasn't born in boardrooms or leadership books. It emerged in 19th-century aesthetics, coined by philosopher Robert Vischer in 1873 to describe how we "feel into" a sculpture or painting. His term carried a quiet revolution: empathy not as performance, but as projection (of presence, of aliveness) into the form of another.

Theodor Lipps extended the idea (Lipps, 1903). We come to know others not by analyzing them, but by resonating with them, mirroring their inner lives subtly and unconsciously. He saw empathy as the mechanism behind not only art appreciation but all interpersonal connection.

Later, Edith Stein, under the guidance of Edmund Husserl, reframed empathy as an intentional act of consciousness: an ethical mode of perceiving the lived experience of another, without fusing or appropriating it (Stein, 1917/1989). For Stein, empathy preserved otherness while affirming connection.

Then came the translation.

In 1909, Edward Titchener translated Einfühlung into the English word "empathy," and something was lost (Zahavi & Rochat, 2015). What had once been a dynamic dance of connection became a frozen skill set. We reduced a relational force to a polite gesture. We made empathy small.

But Einfühlung was never soft. It was sovereign. Radical. Disturbing. Alive.

To reclaim it is not to look back: it's to remember what leadership forgot.

Wisdom Across Traditions

Our modern conception of empathy, with its emphasis on individual feeling states and psychological projection, is remarkably recent. Yet, the fundamental human capacity to sense, understand, and respond to others' experiences has been recognized and cultivated through wisdom traditions for millennia.

Many Indigenous traditions understand what we now call empathy not as psychological projection, but as recognition of fundamental interconnection (Kimmerer, 2013). The Australian Aboriginal practice of dadirri, deep listening, involves a quality of attention that goes beyond hearing words to sensing spirit and the unspoken. As Aboriginal elder Miriam-Rose Ungunmerr-Baumann explains, it is a practice of "deep, inner listening and quiet, still awareness" (Ungunmerr-Baumann, 2002).

This receptive stance contrasts sharply with Western empathy's emphasis on active projection. Instead, dadirri creates space for truth to emerge and be received.

Buddhist psychology grounds compassion (karuna) not in projection but in presence: the capacity to be fully with another's experience without grasping or aversion (Wallace, 2001). Buddhist traditions particularly emphasize integrating compassion with equanimity (upeksha). Unlike Western empathy that can lead to emotional contagion, this balanced approach allows one to remain present with suffering without becoming overwhelmed.

As Vietnamese Zen master Thich Nhat Hanh teaches, "The most precious gift we can offer others is our presence. When mindfulness embraces those we love, they will bloom like flowers" (Hanh, 2014, p. 81).

Presence is empathy's original form. Not projection. Not performance. Just being with.

These traditions suggest that effectiveness lies not in better technique but in deeper presence, not in emotional matching but in ethical relationship, not in occasional states but in continuous awareness.

The Forgotten Signal: Discomfort as Evidence

Perhaps most concerning is how we've sanitized empathy of its discomfort. In leadership contexts especially, empathy has been rebranded as a smooth, frictionless experience—a way to "connect" with others without being disturbed by them.

But genuine empathy is often profoundly uncomfortable.

When you truly encounter another's reality, particularly when that reality challenges your assumptions or implicates you in systems you benefit from, discomfort is not incidental. It is essential.

The discomfort you feel when empathizing across difference isn't a failure of empathy. It's proof that it's working.

As philosopher Emmanuel Levinas argued, the encounter with the Other fundamentally challenges the sovereignty of the self. To truly see another is to be changed by them (Levinas, 1969).

Research by vulnerability expert Brené Brown reveals that leaders who embrace discomfort and uncertainty create more innovative, resilient organizations than those who maintain emotional distance (Brown, 2012). Similarly, adaptive leadership theorist Ronald Heifetz demonstrates that the capacity to "sit with" discomfort during complex challenges is what enables breakthrough solutions (Heifetz, 1994). Far from undermining authority, the willingness to be affected by others' experiences signals the kind of courage that inspires authentic followership.

The leaders who demonstrate true empathic presence are not those with the smoothest technique or the most comfortable demeanor. They are those willing to be disturbed, to have their certainties questioned, their assumptions challenged, and their perspectives expanded through genuine encounter with others.

1.3 Empathy in Motion

Rather than viewing empathy as a static quality—something you either have or don't—we can begin to see it as a dynamic force that moves, adapts, and expresses itself in different ways across contexts.

Empathy is not a noun alone. It is also a verb.

Recent neuroscience research reveals that empathy is deeply rooted in interoception, our ability to sense internal bodily signals like heartbeat, breath, and muscle tension (Ondobaka et al., 2019). The insula, a brain region that processes both bodily awareness and social emotions, lights up during empathic encounters, creating a bridge between what we feel in our bodies and what we understand about others.

Trauma researcher Bessel van der Kolk's work demonstrates how the body holds emotional intelligence that often precedes conscious awareness (van der Kolk, 2014). When we learn to attune to our internal signals, we not only improve our capacity for self-regulation but also enhance our ability to read others' emotional states accurately. This embodied intelligence becomes the foundation for empathic leadership that serves rather than depletes.

Neuroscientist Stephen Porges' Polyvagal Theory shows how our nervous system shifts between different states of engagement and withdrawal, each allowing different degrees and forms of empathic connection (Porges, 2011). When we feel safe, we can engage in complex social emotions and nuanced understanding. When we feel threatened, our capacity for empathic attunement narrows or disappears entirely.

This explains why empathy fades—deeply present one moment, absent the next. Our empathic capacity depends not just on intention, but on nervous system regulation.

Empathy is less like a fixed trait and more like a dance: a dynamic, embodied process of attunement that shifts with context, relationship, and internal state.

The Human Engine: Five Forms of Empathy in Motion

This understanding leads to a fundamental reframing. What if empathy takes different forms depending on what the moment requires? What if its power lies not in its stability, but in its adaptability?

The Human Engine proposes that empathy flows through five interconnected capacities, each addressing different limitations of conventional empathy:

Feel: When we are attuning to our environment or to a team dynamic, empathy shows up as receptive awareness that precedes analysis or judgment. This form is somatic, intuitive, and often pre-verbal, listening not just with the mind, but with the body.

Discern: When evaluating competing demands or setting boundaries, empathy becomes the capacity to distinguish between different needs, values, and possibilities without collapsing into false either/or choices. This directly addresses

11

the bias problem, providing ethical guardrails that pure emotional empathy lacks.

Imagine: When envisioning what does not yet exist, empathy becomes the engine of moral imagination. This form moves beyond present reality to envision what might be, not as escape, but as ethical act.

Respond: When taking bold or compassionate action, empathy expresses itself through the capacity to move from understanding to impact, from knowing to doing. This bridges the gap between awareness and change.

Replenish: When tending to ourselves and others in the aftermath of exertion, loss, or change, empathy becomes the recognition that sustainable impact requires rhythms of renewal. This counteracts empathic distress, ensuring that connection remains energizing rather than depleting.

Together, these five dynamic capacities create a regenerative cycle that keeps people, teams, and systems alive. They are not steps in a process, but living expressions through which empathy is activated, matured, and scaled.

This dynamic model resolves many of the contradictions in how we understand empathy. It explains why empathy can be both emotional and cognitive, both individual and collective, both spontaneous and cultivated. It offers a path beyond both uncritical celebration and wholesale dismissal of empathy as a concept.

The Research Converges

The view of empathy presented here (Einfühlung as dynamic, embodied, and systemic) is no longer fringe theory. Across neuroscience, phenomenology, and systems science, the emerging consensus is clear: empathy is not simply emotional matching or perspective-taking. It is embodied presence. Relational signal. A co-created field of attention and attunement.

Neuroscientist Antonio Damasio showed that our deepest knowing often begins in the body, in the form of somatic markers: pre-verbal signals that shape moral clarity and decision-making (Damasio, 1994). These insights help us remember what Wilhelm Worringer hinted at a century ago: the way we relate to the world, whether through control or connection, shapes what we see, how we lead, and what we create.

Empathy, in this light, is not a soft skill or a fixed trait. It is a system-level intelligence.

Reclaiming Empathy, Remembering Ourselves

So where are we now?

We are returning, not to sentiment, but to source. To an older understanding of empathy, one that began in breath, not branding. In art, not algorithms. In presence, not performance.

Empathy was never just a skill. It was never meant to live in HR manuals or feedback forms. Its root, Einfühlung, asked us to feel into the world, into each other, not from the safety of distance, but from the courage of nearness.

Now, after decades of flattening and professionalizing empathy into something digestible, we are beginning to remember what it really is.

Not soft, but systemic.
Not nice, but necessary.
Not a trait, but a tuning.

This book stands in that remembering. We are no longer debating whether empathy matters: we're reshaping what empathy actually is, and reclaiming it as a relational, systemic, and embodied capacity that leadership cannot afford to ignore.

The Human Engine begins with sensing, but it lives in motion. What follows is an exploration of empathy not as sentiment, but as capacity. A human technology. A design principle. And a leadership stance for our most complex challenges.

This is not a lament. It's a design invitation: to restore what has been numbed, and to remember that empathy, too, can be engineered.

But this reclamation of empathy as Einfühlung raises an immediate question: if empathy isn't performance, how do we actually practice it? The answer begins not in the mind, but in the body—with learning to notice what we feel before we know what it means.

TOOL:
FROM EMPATHY DISPLAY TO EINFÜHLUNG:
A LEADERSHIP PRESENCE AUDIT

Before moving forward, take a moment to assess where you currently stand. This audit will help you notice the difference between empathy as performance and empathy as presence, a distinction that will become crucial as we explore The Human Engine.

Instructions: Rate yourself on a scale of 1-5 for each statement (1 = rarely, 5 = consistently). Look for patterns in your responses. Where do you tend toward performance? Where do you embody presence?

Performance Indicators
- I maintain appropriate facial expressions when listening to difficult feedback ___
- I use phrases like "I understand" even when I'm not fully connecting ___
- I check the time during emotional conversations ___
- I have a repertoire of responses ready for common concerns ___
- I prioritize appearing empathic over being disturbed by others' reality ___
- I feel relieved when emotional moments in meetings end ___

Performance Total: ___/30

Presence Indicators

- I notice my own discomfort when encountering perspectives that challenge mine ___
- I can recall specific details about team members' concerns weeks later ___
- I allow conversations to change me and my decisions ___
- I create unstructured time for connection without agenda ___
- I recognize when I'm emotionally unavailable and adjust accordingly ___
- I'm willing to be visibly affected by others' experiences ___

Presence Total: ___/30

Your Empathy Profile

If your Performance score is higher than your Presence score: You may be relying on learned techniques rather than authentic encounter. Consider: What would it feel like to risk being changed by a conversation?

If your Presence score is higher than your Performance score: You're oriented toward genuine connection. Consider: How can you maintain this authenticity under pressure?

If scores are roughly equal: You're likely code-switching between performance and presence based on context. Consider: What conditions make presence feel safe versus risky?

Strong Presence indicators (24+ points): You demonstrate capacity for Einfühlung: feeling into others while staying grounded in yourself.

Reflection Questions

1. In what contexts do you tend to perform rather than presence?

2. What triggers your shift from genuine encounter to choreographed response?
3. What would it cost you to practice more presence? What might it create?
4. Who in your life models true empathic presence? What can you learn from them?

Remember: The goal is not perfection but awareness. Even the most present leaders sometimes perform. The distinction lies in noticing the difference and cultivating the courage to choose encounter over performance when it matters most.

Chapter 2
BEFORE WE KNOW

The Body's Signal and the Start of Empathy

"The body knows things about which the mind is ignorant."
—Jacques Lecoq

The surgeon's hands froze mid-suture. Something felt wrong. Not with the procedure, but with the patient. The monitors showed stable vitals, the anesthesiologist nodded reassuringly, but her fingers had detected an almost imperceptible change in tissue tension.

"Wait," she said, stepping back. Within minutes, the team discovered internal bleeding that the instruments hadn't yet registered. Her hands had known first.

In a world of data and dashboards, subtle sensing may seem like a luxury. But for leaders, failing to notice early bodily signals can lead to strategic misreads, missed interpersonal cues, and moral drift. The body doesn't just feel. It foresees.

Before you act, even before emotion, there is sensation—the flutter, the shift, the whisper beneath thought.

Empathy is a trained perceptual capacity. This chapter explores how our bodies become instruments of empathy, registering what matters before we know why it matters. To lead well, we must first learn to notice.

What have you felt in your body lately that you didn't speak aloud? What's your relationship to early signals? Do you notice them, dismiss them, or override them? This chapter invites you to begin again by listening deeper.

2.1 The Signal Before the Story: Why the Body Speaks First

This return to embodied sensing is what Einfühlung originally invited: not emotional projection, but presence that feels into the world through the body's quiet knowing.

If Chapter 1 reclaimed empathy from sentimental caricature, this chapter roots it in the nervous system, where attention, not emotion, is empathy's first frontier.

Empathy doesn't begin in emotion or understanding, it begins in sensation. Signal awareness is the ground on which all other empathic capacities are built. This sensing forms the foundation for a larger cycle of empathic practice that moves through discernment, imagination, response, and renewal—what we'll come to know as the Human Engine. But it all starts here, with the body's quiet knowing beneath the noise.

The Signal Before Words

Elaine felt it first—a flicker in her chest. Nothing dramatic. Just a subtle tightening as her team's senior designer spoke about the project timeline. Around the conference table, faces remained neutral. The quarterly review presentation continued without interruption. By all outward measures, everything was on track.

But the sensation persisted, that subtle internal disruption that couldn't yet form itself into words. The designer's shoulders seemed slightly higher than usual, his typically fluid gestures more contained. When he paused between slides, the silence carried a different quality than his usual thoughtful transitions.

Have you ever felt a subtle dissonance before a meeting went sideways, but couldn't name it in time?

Elaine had learned to trust these moments of internal dissonance. Rather than pushing forward as she might have years ago, she took a slow breath and said, "Something feels off about our timeline. I can't quite put my finger on it yet, but I sense there's something we're missing. What are we not seeing here?"

Her pause made space for the team to compare what they felt with what she had sensed.

For three seconds, nothing happened. Then the designer's posture softened. "I didn't want to derail the presentation," he admitted, "but we've hit unexpected complexity in the user authentication system. The timeline is technically possible, but it would require cutting corners on security testing."

Around the table, other team members began nodding, relief visible as the unspoken concern found voice. What might have become a crisis of rushed implementation or hidden compromises transformed instead into a collaborative problem-solving session, all because Elaine had noticed and honored that first wordless signal.

What Is the Signal?
Signal: A pre-conscious, embodied cue. A tightening in the chest, a flutter in the gut, or a change in breath. These are not yet emotions or stories, but data.

The signal isn't yet emotion (which involves interpretation), not quite intuition (which draws on patterned experience), and certainly not analysis. Unlike intuition, which often relies on accumulated experience, a signal is raw, pre-pattern, pre-story—a first somatic alert that something meaningful is unfolding. Where intuition reflects past pattern recognition, a signal arises before any such pattern has formed, an embodied 'ping' that precedes both memory and meaning.

Three Types of Signal:

1. **Empathic Signals:** Bodily responses to others' unexpressed emotional states or relational dynamics (the flutter when someone is struggling but not saying so)

2. **Ethical Signals:** Physical responses to moral misalignment or values conflicts (the knot in your stomach when a decision feels wrong, even if it's profitable)

3. **Systemic Signals:** Somatic responses to organizational or strategic emergence (the tightness when systems are out of alignment, even if metrics look good)

These signal types reflect established patterns in human perception: empathic signals align with research on mirror neurons that enable us to sense others' unexpressed states; ethical signals echo the pre-conscious moral judgments that guide decision-making; and systemic signals mirror organizational sensemaking, where leaders detect misalignment before it becomes explicit.

All three types share common characteristics: they emerge before conscious analysis, they carry information about what matters, and they invite attention rather than immediate action.

Signal ≠ Emotion

- Signal: A raw, pre-conscious bodily cue (tightness, flutter, stillness)
- Emotion: A meaning-laden state (anxiety, joy) that often follows signal + interpretation

Signals invite attention before interpretation—they're data, not conclusions.

The signal is not the event. It's the early stir that tells you something matters.

The Signal-to-Action Framework

Signal (preconscious) → Interoceptive noticing (conscious) → Narrative framing (cognitive meaning-making) → Discernment (ethical/empathic reflection) → Action (response)

Without honoring this sequence, leadership becomes reactive rather than wise.

"The signal is not noise. It is early truth."

For leaders like Elaine, these fleeting sensations offer invaluable intelligence that often precedes analytical understanding. But in dominant institutional contexts, particularly in Western business culture, these subtle signals are routinely dismissed or overridden, often at tremendous cost to connection, insight, and ultimately, results.

These somatic cues are not just background noise. They are ignition points, the first gear of the Human Engine that allows all other empathic capacities to engage.

This capacity to sense signals becomes the foundation for what we'll explore as the FEEL capacity of the Human Engine: the ability to detect what matters before it becomes crisis.

The signal isn't separate from thought or action. It's the system's first stir.

Wholeness isn't an abstract ideal—it's how insight begins, how a system stirs before it speaks. To ignore the signal is not only to dismiss the body, it is to fragment the self.

2.2 Why We Miss the Signal: States and Stress

Why Presence Is Physiology

Understanding the neurobiological conditions that either support or inhibit our capacity to notice signals helps explain why this early form of awareness can be so elusive, especially in high-pressure environments. Empathic leadership doesn't begin with action or even insight. It begins with perception, specifically, the body's ability to register what matters before the mind can name it.

Our nervous system constantly shifts between different physiological states that dramatically affect what we can perceive. Neuroscientist Stephen Porges' Polyvagal Theory outlines three primary autonomic states that shape our capacity for connection and signal detection (Porges, 2011):

- **Ventral Vagal:** Safe, socially engaged. When we feel safe, the parasympathetic nervous system supports social engagement and fine-tuned perception. In this state, we are most capable of sensing subtle emotional and relational signals.
- **Sympathetic:** Fight or flight. When we detect danger or urgency, the sympathetic nervous system activates our fight-or-flight response. Our attention narrows, focused on immediate survival rather than nuance or social complexity.
- **Dorsal Vagal:** Freeze and withdrawal. Under conditions of overwhelming threat, the nervous system may shut

down entirely. This freeze response leads to disconnection, numbing, and diminished access to both self-awareness and empathy.

While aspects of Polyvagal Theory remain debated in the scientific community, its framework offers a valuable lens for understanding how physiological state influences signal awareness and social engagement.

Most organizational environments inadvertently encourage sympathetic activation: performance pressure, tight deadlines, nonstop meetings, and hyper-responsiveness. Ironically, these are the very conditions under which signals are most critical, and most likely to be missed.

Porges observes that in states of threat, our neuroception detects features of risk and our nervous system shifts accordingly to support survival rather than social engagement (Porges, 2011, p. 123).

The executive racing from meeting to meeting, the team scrambling toward a deadline, the organization facing crisis: each operates in a physiological state that suppresses subtle sensing in favor of reactive functioning.

Elaine had no language for Polyvagal states, but she knew what it meant to pause when her chest spoke louder than the slides. That momentary tightness was her nervous system registering what her conscious mind hadn't yet processed: a misalignment between words and reality that would have derailed the project if left unaddressed.

This isn't about personal failure. It's about misaligned systems. We've built leadership cultures that demand constant urgency, then expect grounded awareness and insight on command. But biology doesn't work that way. When we live in reactivity, we lose access to the very intelligence that enables wise leadership (Arnsten, 2009).

2.3 Training the Instrument: Interoception and Empathic Accuracy

Beyond nervous system states, our access to subtle signals depends on the quality of our interoceptive awareness: our ability to sense internal bodily states. Neuroscientist A.D. Craig describes interoception as the sense of the physiological condition of the body, encompassing awareness of heartbeat, breathing, digestion, muscle tension, and other internal sensations (Craig, 2002).

Research reveals that accurate interoception correlates with emotional intelligence, decision-making quality, and empathic capacity (Critchley & Garfinkel, 2017). The insular cortex, the brain's interoceptive hub, integrates internal sensory input and contributes to the subjective experience of feeling (Craig, 2009). In short, the insula helps us feel what we feel, often before we can name it.

Recent studies demonstrate that interoceptive training (practices that enhance our ability to detect internal bodily signals like heartbeat or breathing patterns) improves both emotional clarity and empathic accuracy while reducing empathic distress (Quadt et al., 2022). This research supports what embodied leaders have long intuited: the better we sense our own internal states, the more precisely we can attune to others without becoming overwhelmed.

Somatic signals don't compete with thinking. They deepen it. The most reliable signals emerge when cross-referenced with context and team insights, balancing intuition with analysis.

Despite its importance, interoception is rarely developed in leadership contexts. We train minds to analyze but neglect to train bodies to feel. We develop rigorous frameworks for external assessment but neglect the equally essential capacity to register what's happening within.

Western intellectual traditions have long privileged detached observation over embodied knowing, creating the myth of the mental: the belief that human intelligence resides primarily in abstract reasoning rather than in embodied engagement with the world (Dreyfus, 1992).

Try This: Pause. Name three sensations in your body right now. Don't judge. Just notice.

From Disconnection to Intelligence

Research in embodied cognition offers a corrective to this disembodied view of intelligence. Cognitive scientists like George Lakoff and Mark Johnson demonstrate that even our most abstract concepts are grounded in bodily experience (Lakoff & Johnson, 1999). We understand "relationship" through physical schemas of connection, "progress" through forward movement, "understanding" through seeing or grasping. Our thinking isn't separate from our physicality: it emerges from it.

Consider the product manager who, midway through a client call, feels a sudden heaviness in her chest. The conversation seems fine on the surface, but something isn't resonating. Instead of pushing through, she pauses to ask a clarifying question. The client hesitates, then reveals a key concern that had gone unspoken. Her decision to trust that moment of felt sense, not as a conclusion but as an invitation, reshaped the relationship.

Curiosity doesn't begin with a question. It begins with sensation: a felt sense that something isn't settled, that something matters enough to pause and explore.

Empathy is not emotional labor or performance. It is a way of sensing with accuracy and presence.

Empathy is not the performance of care or the management of others' feelings. It is the capacity to feel without fusing, to sense what is happening in the relational field without losing oneself in others' experience. This distinction is crucial: emotional labor depletes; empathy, when practiced with boundaries, energizes and informs.

For leaders, the body is not merely a vehicle for the mind but an essential instrument of perception. The sensations we feel (the tightness in the chest during a difficult conversation, the expansiveness when encountering an exciting possibility, the subtle contraction when reviewing a troubling report) offer data that complements and often precedes intellectual analysis.

2.4 The Politics of Attention: Whose Signal Gets Heard?

Not all signals are heard. Power influences what gets noticed and what stays invisible.

The capacity to notice and respond to subtle signals isn't equally distributed. It's profoundly shaped by power, privilege, and social location: factors that determine whose cues get noticed and whose remain invisible.

Research by psychologist Dacher Keltner shows that increased power correlates with decreased empathic accuracy: the ability to correctly identify others' emotions and experiences (Keltner, 2016, p. 67). This power paradox means that as leaders gain influence, their perception of subtle cues often diminishes.

Beyond formal power, social privilege creates patterns of selective perception that filter certain signals while amplifying others. Research on motivated perception demonstrates that we literally see what aligns with existing beliefs and interests, while failing to notice what doesn't (Balcetis & Dunning, 2006).

Maya pulled back when the conversation turned to "cultural fit" in hiring. Her shoulders tensed, her contributions became more measured. But the CEO didn't notice her withdrawal. He missed the signal that this seemingly progressive discussion had triggered past experiences of coded exclusion. Maya's hesitation reflects how signals from marginalized voices are often dismissed or unrecognized in organizational settings.

Elaine later reflected: Would Maya have spoken up if she had been newer to the team? Would the signal have been received? Signal literacy isn't just individual: it's shaped by power, position, and the safety to be heard.

This understanding reveals what we might call structural signal suppression: the systematic ways that organizational power dynamics silence certain voices before they can speak. When identities intersect (race and gender, class and sexuality, disability and age) the consequences of signaling become compounded. The cost of speaking up multiplies. The safety to sense diminishes.

Following theorist Sara Ahmed, we can think of signals as emotionally coded, and some bodies are socially permitted to express discomfort, while others are punished or ignored for the same cues (Ahmed, 2010, pp. 41-42). This extends to signals: whose early warnings get heard? Whose discomfort gets dismissed as "sensitivity"? Attention is not neutral. Power determines not just what we see, but what we are allowed to see.

Reflection question: Whose signals do you find easiest to notice? Whose might you be missing because of your position or background?

Reclaiming Signal Intelligence

When we override or ignore the early cues our body sends, we don't just miss information: we miss the foundation for genuine connection, ethical clarity, and sustainable effectiveness. The costs manifest across multiple dimensions:

Strategic blindness: The executive who dismisses the subtle unease when reviewing projections may miss early warning signs of market shifts. Research on strategic intuition by William Duggan suggests that breakthrough insights often begin as subtle, non-verbal patterns recognized below conscious awareness (Duggan, 2007).

Relational disconnection: The team leader who ignores the tension in their body during a difficult conversation misses crucial data about team dynamics. Research on psychological safety demonstrates that leaders who can detect and address subtle signs of discomfort or misalignment before they escalate create environments where teams learn faster, innovate more effectively, and perform at higher levels (Edmondson & Lei, 2014).

Ethical numbing: Perhaps most concerning is how disconnection from internal cues can impair moral perception. The executive who has learned to override the knot in their stomach when implementing difficult decisions may be bypassing vital ethical information.

Personal depletion: Finally, chronic disconnection from bodily signals leads to lost authenticity: a profound alienation from one's own experience that contributes to burnout, health problems, and diminished effectiveness (Maté, 2003, pp. 123-124).

A healthcare administrator learned this lesson painfully. For months, she ignored the knot in her stomach during staff meetings where budget cuts were discussed. "I told myself it was just stress," she reflected. "But my body was registering what my mind couldn't yet face: that these cuts would compromise patient care." When two nurses quit and patient satisfaction scores dropped, she understood: her body had known the human cost before the spreadsheets did.

But empathy can be reclaimed. When we learn to honor these early signals, to trust the wisdom that emerges before words, we access a form of intelligence that transforms how we lead, decide, and connect.

2.5 Practices for Embodied Leadership

Rebuilding connection to early bodily cues requires practices that may seem counterintuitive in conventional leadership contexts:

Creating Attentional Space

The capacity to notice subtle signals requires attention of the highest order: a quality of presence that is both receptive and disciplined (Weil, 1949/2009). Research by neuroscientist Amishi Jha reveals that even brief mindfulness practices significantly enhance attentional control and working memory capacity, key resources for noticing subtle signals (Jha, 2018).

Micro-practices for signal awareness:
- **90-Second Reset**: Scan your body from head to toe. What's tight? What's open? What's asking for attention?
- **Signal Check-ins**: Ask, "What is my body telling me right now?" Notice without analyzing.
- **Somatic Notes**: Track how your body feels during conversations alongside your regular notes.

Developing Interoceptive Awareness

Reconnecting with bodily sensations provides the foundation for early signal recognition. To feel into another, we must first feel into ourselves. Einfühlung begins in the breath before it reaches the boundary of another.

Practices that enhance interoceptive awareness include body scanning, mindful movement, and simple check-ins. Psychiatrist Bessel van der Kolk found that regular practices that enhance body awareness significantly improve emotional regulation, decision-making, and interpersonal effectiveness (van der Kolk, 2014).

Building your signal vocabulary:
- **Expansion vs. Contraction**: Notice when your body opens or closes in response to ideas, people, or situations
- **Energy Quality**: Track whether interactions leave you energized, drained, or neutral
- **Boundary Signals**: Pay attention to sensations that signal when something feels "off" relationally or ethically

Supporting Nervous System Regulation
Creating conditions that support ventral vagal activation involves practices that signal safety to the nervous system: conscious breathing, grounding through sensory awareness, and co-regulation (the calming effect of being in the presence of another regulated nervous system).

Environmental signal support:
- Design physical spaces that support nervous system regulation (natural elements, appropriate lighting, spaces for movement)
- Create meeting rhythms that allow for transition time between intense conversations
- Practice co-regulation by maintaining your own grounded presence during difficult discussions

Embodied Leadership in Action
Leaders who integrate somatic awareness into their practice report measurable improvements in team trust, strategic clarity,

and organizational resilience. Research on embodied leadership reveals that leaders trained in body-based practices, including the signal detection techniques outlined above, enhance their capacity for presence and decision-making while strengthening team alignment (Ladkin, 2021).

These practices aren't merely personal development; they're strategic investments. When leaders learn to sense systemic stress, ethical misalignment, or relational tension through their bodies, they can address challenges before they escalate into crises.

A senior VP once told me how he ignored the knot in his stomach before approving a cost-cutting measure. Three months later, when key talent left and morale plummeted, he understood what his body had been trying to tell him: the numbers worked, but the human cost was too high. "I knew," he said. "My body knew before my spreadsheet did."

Months later, Elaine began starting team meetings with a simple check-in: "What's your body telling you about this project?" What once felt too vague or soft was now becoming a valued form of early leadership insight. Her team discovered that their collective signals often pointed toward issues their analysis hadn't yet surfaced. Signal literacy had become a team competency, not just an individual practice.

Shared sensing is not soft. It defines what's possible.

The Path Forward: From Sensing to Systems
The early signal represents the earliest stage of empathic awareness: the moment when something registers as significant before we can fully articulate why. It is the beginning of a larger cycle of empathic practice that integrates perception with discernment, imagination, response, and renewal: the Human Engine we'll explore in the coming chapters.

But it begins here, with noticing, with the courage to feel what is happening before rushing to fix, define, or control it. In a culture that prizes certainty and solution, this receptive attention may be the most radical act of all.

Before insight speaks in sentences, it stirs in cells. The body knows. Your attention is the invitation.

The leaders who will thrive in our complex future are not those with the quickest answers but those with the deepest capacity to sense what is emerging before it can be named, and to stay present with that emergence long enough for genuine wisdom to arise.

When these early signals are received, honored, and acted upon, the Human Engine begins to turn. Empathy doesn't just 'show up': it activates, cell by cell, breath by breath. What we've learned to notice in ourselves becomes the foundation for sensing patterns in teams, organizations, and systems.

Individual signal awareness, however, is just the beginning. The real transformation happens when one person's sensing (like Elaine's recognition that 'something feels off') becomes permission for collective wisdom to emerge. When personal signals scale into organizational intelligence, empathy becomes competitive advantage.

TOOL
SIGNAL JOURNAL:
A WEEK OF SOMATIC NOTICING

Empathy begins as signal, not story. This tool helps you practice that pre-narrative noticing. The better you track it, the more fluent you become in the early language of leadership.

Purpose: To strengthen your capacity to notice and work with subtle internal signals before they develop into fully conscious awareness.

Instructions: For one week, use this simple tracking practice to become more aware of your signals. Use a phone note, journaling app, or even voice memos if writing slows you down.

1. **Set Intention:** Each **morning**, take 30 seconds to set an intention to notice subtle internal signals throughout the day.
2. **Track Moments:** When you **notice** a signal—a subtle bodily sensation that signals something significant—briefly note:
   - What was happening when you noticed it
   - Where you felt it in your body
   - The quality of the sensation (e.g., tightness, warmth, heaviness)
   - The type of signal (empathic, ethical, or systemic)
   - Whether you followed or overrode the signal
   - What happened as a result
3. **Sample Tracking Format:**

Situation	Bodily Sensation	Quality	Signal Type	Response	Outcome
Budget meeting when CFO	Flutter in stomach	Fluttery, unstable	Systemic	Paused, asked	Discovered critical resource gap

Situation	Bodily Sensation	Quality	Signal Type	Response	Outcome
questioned timeline				clarifying question	
Email from key client	Tightness in chest	Constricted, shallow breathing	Empathic	Ignored it, sent quick reply	Missed important subtext, had to revisit issue
Team member's presentation	Expansion in chest	Warm, open	Empathic	Gave positive feedback	Strengthened team member's confidence

4. **End-of-Week Reflection:**

o What patterns do you notice in when and where you experience signals?

o Which bodily sensations are most common for you?

o Which type of signal (empathic, ethical, systemic) do you notice most/least?

o What happens when you honor these signals? What happens when you override them?

o How might you create more space to notice and honor these signals in the coming week?

Remember: The goal isn't to analyze these sensations immediately, but to strengthen your capacity to notice them. With practice, you'll develop greater fluency in this pre-verbal intelligence that often precedes your most important insights.

Chapter 3
Empathy as Infrastructure

How Individual Sensing Becomes Organizational Intelligence

"The health of a system depends on the capacity of its parts to sense and respond to each other."
— Daniel Schmachtenberger

The boardroom fell silent. Sarah, the VP of Product, had just asked the question no one else would: "What if we're solving the wrong problem?"

Six months into a major platform redesign—with millions invested and tight deadlines looming—Sarah suggested a pivot. Not because the technology failed, but because they'd finally heard users' voices in late-night support tickets, frustrated forum posts, and hesitant interview pauses.

The CEO shifted in his chair. The CFO pulled up budget projections. But something had already shifted in the room. Sarah wasn't just raising a concern; she was revealing a pattern they'd all sensed but hadn't named. The company's entire strategy had been built on assumptions about user behavior that no longer held true.

What happened next would determine whether this organization could adapt, or whether it would join the graveyard of companies that mistook their maps for the territory, like Kodak, blinded by film-era assumptions.

Sarah's moment wasn't just about courage—it was about signal processing becoming system intelligence. What her organization did next illustrates how empathy becomes a dynamic capability.

Too often, empathy is treated as a personality trait or an interpersonal bonus. But what if it's something deeper—a sensing technology that enables organizational adaptation? This chapter explores how individual signal awareness scales into collective intelligence, creating a "dynamic capability": the capacity to sense, seize, and transform in response to changing conditions.

Empathy isn't a soft skill. It's sensing infrastructure—subtle, fast, and deeply attuned to human systems. Empathy doesn't replace data, it amplifies it, catching nuances that metrics miss until crises emerge. The organizations that will thrive in our complex future aren't those with the quickest answers, but those with the deepest capacity to sense what's emerging before it shows up in the data (Teece, 2007).

Yet this isn't about emotional labor or performing care. Research shows that emotional intelligence scales in diverse teams through specific practices and measurable outcomes: team cohesion, innovation rates, reduced turnover (Ashkanasy et al., 2002). We're talking about precision sensing that serves performance, not sentiment.

The cost of missing these signals is stark: Wells Fargo's fraudulent accounts scandal wasn't a failure of information—it was a failure to feel what was happening to customers and employees (Warren,

2017). Boeing's 737 MAX crashes weren't just engineering failures, they were sensing failures—an inability to detect mounting safety concerns before they became catastrophic (Robison, 2019).

But when individual sensing becomes organizational sensing, something powerful emerges: empathic sensing as competitive advantage.

3.1 From Individual Signal to Collective Intelligence

Sarah's moment of recognizing 'something feels off' exemplifies the signal awareness we explored in Chapter 2, but here we see how individual sensing becomes collective intelligence.

How does one person's sensing become a system's adaptive capacity?

Empathy doesn't scale by addition. It scales by resonance.

In that boardroom, the moment after Sarah spoke, something shifted. Sarah had activated FEEL: the capacity to detect early signals before they calcify into crises. Her subtle sensing of user misalignment had preceded any metric showing declining satisfaction.

The head of customer success hesitated, then pulled up a dashboard showing a spike in support tickets—complaints about "feature overload" that had been categorized as user error. The lead engineer cleared his throat and admitted he'd been getting questions from the QA team about whether the interface was "too complex for regular users." The marketing director, who'd been silent, finally shared feedback from focus groups that hadn't made it into official reports: "Users feel overwhelmed within minutes of logging in."

What seemed like individual anxiety turned out to be collective wisdom waiting for permission. Sarah's question didn't just surface information—it created co-regulation. Her willingness to voice uncertainty gave others permission to share their own doubts.

The Neuroscience of Collective Wisdom

This is social resonance: the capacity for a group's nervous systems to synchronize, creating shared sensing that's more accurate than any individual perspective. Nervous systems align, enhancing cognition for ambiguous signals (Siegel, 2012; Hasson et al., 2012).

Research demonstrates how social brains synchronize during group interactions through neural mirroring and limbic resonance, though the precise mechanisms of mirror neuron systems remain actively debated in neuroscience (Cozolino, 2014).

Here's the contrarian insight: the synchronized nervous systems of Sarah's team became more intelligent than any individual brain in that room. Unlike emotional contagion, where stress spreads unconsciously through a system (Barsade, 2002), social resonance is intentional attunement that amplifies collective intelligence.

The Process of Collective Sensing

Sarah's breakthrough hinged on three conditions that transformed individual doubt into organizational wisdom:

Permission to sense: The CEO invited uncomfortable truths without penalty. When Sarah voiced her concern, he could have responded defensively. Instead, he leaned forward and asked, "What are you sensing that we're missing?" Research shows that emotionally intelligent leaders foster "socially intelligent" organizations by modeling regulated responses that create space for collective sensing (Goleman & Boyatzis, 2008).

Capacity to receive: The team's regulated nervous systems shifted from defensiveness to curiosity. The CFO's initial budget anxiety gave way to engagement as he realized the cost of continuing might exceed the cost of pivoting. This neurobiological shift from threat detection to social engagement is what enabled collective intelligence to emerge.

Structure for integration: Whiteboard mapping revealed patterns no individual saw. Within an hour, they'd connected signals across departments and identified a fundamental misalignment between user needs and product assumptions.

The team paused the redesign and interviewed 50 users over the next week. What they discovered challenged conventional product development wisdom: users didn't need more features. They needed confidence. The preference for simplicity over feature density revealed a deeper truth about user psychology that traditional analytics had missed.

Now came the crucial moment: DISCERN. Sarah's team faced a classic leadership dilemma that required navigating competing values and emotions. Protect the six months of investment and engineering work, or serve user needs? This wasn't just analytical—it required both rigorous thinking and values clarity. The team chose user-centricity even when it meant admitting previous mistakes, demonstrating discernment in action.

Despite initial resistance from engineers accustomed to feature-heavy designs, the pivot felt inevitable once the collective sensing was complete.

Sarah's experience isn't unique to technology companies. This pattern of empathic sensing driving strategic advantage extends across industries where human complexity shapes outcomes. Across sectors, leaders who cultivate collective sensing capabilities discover strategic insights that purely analytical approaches miss.

The Six-Month Test: When Sensing Becomes Strategic Advantage

Six months after launch, the real test came. The redesigned platform was technically successful and user reviews were positive, but adoption lagged despite strong word-of-mouth. Traditional metrics showed engagement, but something felt off to the team's newly developed sensing capacity.

This time, the organization's response was different. Instead of defaulting to marketing pushes or feature additions, Sarah's team activated their sensing infrastructure. Cross-functional workshops revealed a pattern across three seemingly unrelated signals: support tickets mentioning "overwhelming options," sales conversations where prospects asked about "simpler alternatives," and user forum posts requesting "getting started" guides.

This collective resonance, enabled by synchronized nervous systems and open dialogue, uncovered a truth no single metric could capture: their platform's richness was paralyzing new users.

Here, the team activated IMAGINE: envisioning alternatives to current patterns. Rather than defaulting to the obvious solutions (more tutorials or customer support) they reimagined their entire onboarding philosophy. They introduced "progressive revelation," a staged experience that gradually exposed functionality based on user readiness and confidence levels. This creative leap moved them beyond "either/or" thinking to discover a "third way" solution that honored both user simplicity and platform capability.

But imagination without action is just wishful thinking. Sarah's sensing only mattered because the team could RESPOND with speed and alignment, restructuring their approach without bureaucratic paralysis. They developed insight-to-action protocols that could activate within days rather than quarters.

The strategic impact was profound. Not only did user adoption accelerate by 60%, but the company discovered a new market segment: organizations that needed powerful tools but lacked technical sophistication. This insight eventually drove 40% of company revenue within two years, creating a competitive moat that competitors couldn't replicate because they lacked the sensing infrastructure to detect such nuanced user needs.

Critically, the team also practiced REPLENISH: building explicit recovery time into their revised timeline and recognizing that sustainable performance requires systematic restoration. Rather than pushing through exhaustion after the intensive user research and rapid pivot, they created space for the team to process the change and restore their capacity for continued adaptation.

The key lesson: Individual signal detection had become an organizational competitive advantage through a systematic cycle of sensing and response. Unlike Theranos, where dissent was silenced until collapse, or Enron, where groupthink prevented anyone from questioning fundamental assumptions, Sarah's team created an infrastructure where signals could surface, integrate, and inform strategy before crisis struck.

3.2 The Architecture of Collective Sensing

What makes sensing travel through systems instead of getting trapped?

Every organization has regulators—people who shape whether signals flow or get filtered out. They may not appear on the org chart, but they determine whether collective intelligence emerges or individual insights die in isolation.

Maya: The Informal Regulator in Action

In Sarah's company, the transformation deepened when they recognized Maya, a senior designer, as a natural regulator. Maya had no management authority, but when she spoke in meetings, people listened differently. When she seemed agitated, the whole team's energy shifted. When she was calm, complex problems felt solvable.

Rather than ignoring this informal influence, leadership made it explicit. They asked Maya to begin important meetings with a brief "energy read," sharing what she sensed in the room before diving into agenda items.

The impact was immediate. In one strategy session, Maya noted a "restless, scattered" energy that felt different from the typical pre-meeting buzz. She invited the team to pause and address what felt unspoken. This simple intervention uncovered a critical miscommunication about project scope, where different departments were operating from incompatible assumptions. What might have festered as background tension became explicit dialogue that saved weeks of misdirected effort and prevented a potential quarter-derailing crisis.

Maya became a "Regulator of Resonance": someone whose nervous system naturally creates conditions for collective sensing. Unlike typical influencers who shape decisions, regulators shape conditions. Regulators don't control direction. They shape conditions. This aligns with adaptive leadership research on "holding environment" leaders who regulate group anxiety during change, enabling teams to stay connected to reality rather than defaulting to defensive patterns (Heifetz et al., 2009).

Here's the uncomfortable truth most organizations miss: these informal regulators often have more influence on team effectiveness than formal managers. Yet, they're rarely recognized, supported, or developed systematically.

To identify your informal regulators, look for those whose presence shifts the room—colleagues who calm chaos or amplify clarity, even without formal authority.

Microclimates of Safety: Making Sensing Possible

Social resonance doesn't emerge automatically. It requires "microclimates of safety": localized conditions where nervous systems can regulate and collective sensing becomes possible. Sarah's team learned to foster four essential conditions:

Psychological Safety: Norms let juniors challenge assumptions ("That's an important signal, tell us more"). Research emphasizes that psychological safety requires emotional courage—the willingness to be vulnerable (Brown, 2018).

Conflict Repair: Brief debriefs after tension acknowledge missteps and rebuild trust, making risk-taking safer over time.

Physiological Calm: The nervous system state that enables social engagement. Before tough discussions, they incorporated 30-second pauses to let nervous systems settle, shifting teams from reactive to receptive states. This simple practice allowed people to access their capacity for nuanced thinking rather than defaulting to survival responses.

Inclusive Attention: The collective focus that emerges when people feel heard and valued, especially recognizing that diverse nervous systems contribute different forms of sensing intelligence. Round-robin check-ins ensured every voice shaped the conversation rather than competing for airtime. Sarah's team learned that their strongest insights often came from voices that didn't fit dominant cultural norms.

These practices transform individual signals into systemic wisdom (Dana, 2018). Unlike Volkswagen, where silenced engineers hid emissions issues until billions were lost (Ewing,

2017), these microclimates enabled Maya's regulatory influence to amplify signals that data alone couldn't capture.

Yet empathic practices face predictable resistance. Research indicates that 52% of employees believe their company's efforts to be empathetic toward employees are dishonest, suggesting challenges in managerial adoption of authentic empathic practices (Ernst & Young, 2023). To counter this skepticism, leaders can pilot sensing sessions in small teams, building trust through early wins. Research shows that change initiatives achieve 70% higher adoption when incrementally implemented (Kotter, 1996). The cost of neglecting these practices is stark: Uber's 2017 culture crisis demonstrated how ignored employee signals about harassment and toxicity led to widespread reputational damage and leadership upheaval that could have been prevented through systematic sensing infrastructure.

While some leaders dismiss empathic practices as intangible, research shows that psychological safety and positive practices drive measurable outcomes like innovation, retention, and organizational agility (Edmondson, 2018; Cameron, 2012).

3.3 Designing for Resonance, Not Chaos

How do we build feedback loops that amplify wisdom instead of reactivity?

The difference between adaptive and fragile organizations often comes down to feedback loop design. Adaptive systems create multiple channels for information to flow. They reward truth-telling and penalize silence about important problems. Fragile systems amplify problems through silence and denial.

Here's the counterintuitive principle: Adaptive organizations seek discomfort. They surface weak signals before they become strong shocks.

Learning from High-Reliability Organizations

Organizations that operate in high-stakes environments (nuclear power plants, aircraft carriers, emergency rooms) have mastered "mindful organizing" (Weick & Sutcliffe, 2015). These high-reliability organizations (HROs) combine collective sensing with rapid response, creating sensing that drives action.

At Pixar, "Braintrust" meetings create a feedback loop where candid critique surfaces weak signals about story quality, enabling course-corrections before films falter (Catmull & Wallace, 2014). Directors present work-in-progress to peers who offer unflinching feedback. The key: comments focus on the work, not the person, and directors retain final decision-making authority.

Sarah's team launched sensing sessions to catch issues before they calcified. In one memorable session, a junior engineer shared an observation that seemed minor: "My mom tried our app and gave up in thirty seconds—said it felt like homework." This signal about onboarding confusion led to a simplified feature set that saved $200,000 in development costs by preventing a complex feature rollout that users couldn't navigate.

Building Response Readiness

The most adaptive organizations link sensing directly to action through "response readiness": pre-established protocols that activate when certain signals appear. Sarah's company developed specific triggers: when customer complaints spike 10% above baseline, a cross-functional review launches within 48 hours. When three or more team members surface similar concerns in sensing sessions, leadership dedicates the next weekly meeting to exploring the pattern.

This isn't bureaucracy—it's organizational immune system design. Like biological systems that recognize threats and mount responses automatically, these organizations don't need extensive deliberation before acting on clear sensing data. Research describes this as creating "learning organizations" through balancing feedback loops that prevent echo chambers and enable rapid course correction (Senge, 2006).

The contrast with fragile systems is stark. Bad news gets filtered out as it moves up hierarchies. Leaders become isolated in optimistic bubbles while frontline reality deteriorates. When crises finally surface, they feel sudden and catastrophic, though warning signs were present for months.

Sarah's sensing infrastructure prevented this pattern. The protocols they developed ensured signals drove action before crises erupted, creating early warning intelligence that became a sustainable competitive advantage.

EMPATHY AT SCALE: THE UNILEVER TRANSFORMATION

Empathy doesn't scale through sentiment. It scales through structure.

While Sarah's team sensed user needs before metrics registered them, Paul Polman's transformation of Unilever demonstrates empathic infrastructure at global scale. During his decade as CEO, Polman dismantled the logic of quarterly capitalism to reorient the company around long-term sustainability, stakeholder well-being, and planetary boundaries.

His approach wasn't ideological—it was empathic sensing applied to business strategy.

Under Polman's leadership, Unilever launched the Sustainable Living Plan, systematically reducing environmental impact while increasing social benefit across its global supply chain. What made this radical wasn't just its ambition but its architecture. Empathy became a design principle embedded in organizational systems.

Sensing Beyond Shareholders: While competitors optimized for quarterly earnings, Polman's Unilever developed sensing capacity for stakeholders traditional business models ignore: future generations, smallholder farmers, communities affected by climate change, workers in supply chains. This wasn't corporate social responsibility—it was sensing advantage.

Early Warning Intelligence: By feeling into what planetary and social systems needed rather than just what financial markets demanded, Unilever identified risks and opportunities competitors missed. They detected consumer shifts toward sustainable

48

products years before market research caught up. They sensed regulatory changes around plastic waste and carbon emissions before policies were enacted.

Response Infrastructure: The Sustainable Living Plan created protocols for acting on these signals. When sensing revealed deforestation in palm oil supply chains, Unilever didn't just change suppliers—they redesigned entire sourcing systems. When they sensed growing water scarcity, they didn't just reduce usage—they reimagined product formulations.

Measurable Impact: Under Polman's leadership, Unilever's sustainable living brands grew faster than the traditional portfolio, demonstrating that empathic sensing drives performance, not just purpose (Polman & Winston, 2021). The company's ability to sense and respond to stakeholder needs before they became market demands created sustainable competitive advantage.

"The biggest deficit in leadership today is not intelligence or knowledge, but empathy and moral courage," Polman observed in *Net Positive*. This exemplifies empathy as dynamic capability: the organizational capacity to sense what systems usually suppress and respond before damage becomes crisis.

Polman's Unilever demonstrates that empathic infrastructure scales not through individual traits but through systematic design. Like Sarah's team sensing user needs, Unilever sensed planetary and social needs—then built organizational capabilities to respond at the speed of emerging challenges rather than the pace of traditional business cycles.

3.4 The Human Engine: Systematizing Empathic Intelligence

How do we turn breakthrough moments into repeatable capabilities?

Sarah's spontaneous insight wasn't accidental. It reflected a repeatable pattern—what this book calls the Human Engine.

The framework draws from complexity science: like adaptive cycles in natural systems, organizations must cycle through exploration, exploitation, and renewal to avoid collapse (Holling, 2001). The Human Engine provides the sensing and response capabilities that enable this adaptive cycling through five interconnected capacities:

FEEL emerged when Sarah detected user misalignment through subtle cues before metrics registered declining satisfaction. Her team learned to notice what traditional analytics missed: the pause before a user clicked, the hesitation in a customer call, the energy shift when certain features were mentioned. This capacity transforms leaders from reactive responders to early warning systems.

DISCERN activated when Sarah's team navigated the competing demands of past investment versus user needs. Complex domains require sensing and experimentation rather than rigid analysis (Snowden & Boone, 2007). This capacity enables teams to hold multiple truths simultaneously and choose wisely when values collide.

IMAGINE drove the team's creative leap to "progressive revelation" rather than defaulting to conventional solutions like more tutorials. This capacity moves teams beyond present constraints to envision what could be—not as escape from reality but as ethical expansion of possibility.

RESPOND ensured that insight translated into swift organizational action through insight-to-action protocols that could activate within days rather than quarters. This capacity bridges the gap between empathic awareness and competitive advantage.

REPLENISH maintained team sustainability by building recovery time into intensive change processes, recognizing that continuous adaptation requires systematic restoration. Research on compassion-based practices shows that organizations that systematically replenish collective capacity outperform those that treat empathy as an unlimited resource (Worline & Dutton, 2017).

Each capacity strengthens the others. Remove one, and the system loses coherence. Sarah's FEEL sparked team DISCERNMENT about priorities, which enabled them to IMAGINE new approaches, RESPOND with agility, and REPLENISH their capacity for continued adaptation.

The Human Engine's cycle mirrors empirically validated team dynamics. Research shows that teams with high social sensitivity (FEEL/DISCERN) and coordinated action (RESPOND) achieve 20% higher performance (Woolley et al., 2010). Studies emphasize structured reflection (REPLENISH) for sustained success (Hackman, 2002). This framework integrates these findings, enabling organizations to systematically sense and adapt, as Sarah's team demonstrated by detecting user needs before metrics.

By understanding empathy as this dynamic system rather than a single trait, organizations can build "sensing advantage": the capacity to detect and adapt to change before it shows up in traditional metrics. These capacities, explored in depth in coming chapters, equip teams to navigate disruptions from market shifts to internal conflicts with both agility and wisdom.

3.5 From Sensing to Strategy: The Contrarian Advantage

Sarah's transformation made her company a sensing organization. As the CEO noted: "Empathy isn't niceness, it's truth. It keeps us grounded when illusions tempt." Quarterly listening labs drew talent to a firm feeling the future.

Here's the contrarian insight that most leaders miss: in a world obsessed with speed and scale, the ultimate competitive advantage may be the capacity to slow down and sense. While competitors rushed to add features, Sarah's team learned to subtract. While others optimized for engagement metrics, they optimized for user confidence. While others chased growth, Sarah's team chased understanding.

This is the promise of empathy as dynamic capability: This isn't about making decisions easier. It's about making them wiser. Not that it eliminates complexity, but that it enables navigation. Not that it guarantees success, but that it maintains connection to reality while pursuing it.

Empathy drives measurable business outcomes. Research found that organizations with empathic practices (FEEL/RESPOND) achieve up to 20% higher profitability and 15% lower turnover (Cameron et al., 2004). Sarah's team, by sensing user needs early, not only boosted adoption by 60% but also secured 40% of revenue from a new market.

Empathic sensing amplifies data, catching nuances metrics miss until it's too late. Sarah's question sparked a strategy that felt market shifts before competitors saw them in analytics, proving that sensing is the ultimate edge in a complex world. Research on positive organizational scholarship shows that practices grounded in human connection and wisdom consistently outperform those based solely on efficiency and competition (Cameron, 2012).

When individual sensing becomes organizational sensing, something powerful emerges: the capacity to feel the future before it arrives. In a world where change happens faster than traditional planning cycles, this sensing advantage may be the most important competitive capability of all.

What Sarah felt that day wasn't a hunch—it was the first breath of an emergent intelligence. The question isn't whether your organization has this capacity. The question is whether you're designing for it.

Yet even the most sophisticated sensing practices will fail if they're planted in hostile soil. Sarah's breakthrough was possible only because her organization had created conditions where speaking uncomfortable truths was safe. Before we can activate the Human Engine, we must examine the ground it requires to grow.

TOOL
SENSING SESSION PROTOCOL

Purpose: Create structured opportunities for weak signals to surface and integrate into organizational intelligence.

When to Use: Monthly team meetings, project milestones, quarterly planning, or when facing unclear situations.

Sarah's Success Example: In one session, her team's junior engineer shared: "My mom tried our app and gave up in thirty seconds." This seemingly minor signal led to simplified onboarding that saved $200,000 in unnecessary feature development.

The Research Foundation: Studies show that structured empathy practices create measurable improvements in team resilience and organizational adaptability (Worline & Dutton, 2017). The Sensing Session Protocol formalizes sensemaking, where structured reflection helps teams detect weak signals, improving decision accuracy by 15% (Weick, 1995). Sarah's $200,000 cost-saving simplification shows how such practices turn collective sensing into strategic advantage, enhancing organizational adaptability.

Basic Structure (20 minutes):

1. Regulation (3 minutes)

- 60 seconds of synchronized breathing to shift into receptive state
- Brief check-in: one word describing current state (no explanation needed)
- Research note: This activates ventral vagal states that enable social engagement (Dana, 2018)

2. Signal Sharing (10 minutes)

- Each person shares one signal they've noticed (something that felt significant but might not show up in metrics)
- Use phrases like "I'm sensing..." or "Something feels off about..."
- No immediate analysis or problem-solving
- Simple acknowledgment: "I hear that signal"
- Include diverse sensing styles: visual patterns, energy shifts, cultural cues, systemic tensions

3. Pattern Recognition (5 minutes)

- What themes emerge across multiple signals?
- Where do individual observations connect?
- What's asking for attention across the system?
- Honor different processing styles: some people see patterns visually, others feel them somatically

4. Integration (2 minutes)

- What does this collective sensing suggest?
- What deserves further exploration?
- Who will carry these insights forward into action?

Advanced Facilitation Notes:

- Assign a facilitator to ensure no one dominates and all signals are heard
- Redirect personal critiques to problem-focused questions: "How does this signal impact our goal?"
- Focus on the work and patterns, not personalities
- Decision-makers retain authority while gaining collective insight
- Document patterns for organizational memory and trend analysis
- Accommodate neurodiverse processing: some participants may need written reflection time before sharing

Cultural Considerations:

- In high-context cultures, pay attention to what's not said—pauses, energy shifts, subtle nonverbals
- Create multiple ways to contribute: verbal sharing, written input, visual mapping
- Recognize that different cultural backgrounds bring different sensing capabilities

Key Principles:

- Signal first, solution later
- Trust collective wisdom over individual certainty
- Create safety for uncomfortable truths
- Build sensing memory across sessions
- Honor diverse forms of intelligence

Empathic sensing is not just an individual capacity—it is the pulse of an adaptive organization. When leaders cultivate conditions where signals flow, resonance emerges. What begins as a flicker of insight can grow into shared understanding, wise strategy, and sustained performance. But only if we listen. The tools we've explored are not the end of the story. They are openings—ways to bring sensing to life in teams and systems. The chapters ahead explore how these rhythms scale. Not through mandates or mechanics, but through leaders willing to design for resonance.

Chapter 4

THE GROUND WE STAND ON

Designing the Conditions for Connection and Care

"You can't grow an oak tree in a desert. And you can't grow empathy in a system that punishes care."
—Margaret Wheatley

Rachel's experience shows that reclaiming Einfühlung (Chapter 1) and cultivating signal awareness (Chapter 2) both depend on environments where care is safe, not punished.

Empathy doesn't emerge through training. It blooms when systems dare to make caring safe.

Rachel's story isn't unique. It's systemic. Across organizations worldwide, naturally empathic people find themselves adapting to environments that make caring professionally dangerous. We've built systems that extract empathy while refusing to sustain it, then wonder why engagement plummets and innovation stalls. But what if the issue isn't a lack of empathy—but that we've designed it out of our organizations?

This chapter explores empathy as an emergent property: a capacity that blooms only when environmental conditions support it. Like a plant that needs specific soil, water, and light to flourish, empathy requires particular organizational nutrients: agency to act on what we sense, efficacy to translate caring into meaningful change, and connection that makes vulnerability safe. When these conditions exist, even moderately caring people become remarkably empathic. When they don't, our most compassionate leaders learn to hide their humanity.

The work ahead requires this foundation. Without environments that welcome empathy, even the most sophisticated practices become performance rather than authentic care.

4.1 The Ground We Stand On

The message came during Rachel's commute: "Emergency all-hands. Budget crisis. Need immediate cost cuts." As the newly appointed head of customer experience at a mid-sized software company, Rachel had joined six months earlier with genuine excitement about building more human-centered practices. She believed deeply in treating both employees and customers with dignity and care.

But as she sat in the emergency meeting that morning, watching colleagues present spreadsheets that reduced human beings to cost centers, something in her began to shut down—not from lack of care, but from the realization that caring might be dangerous here.

"I remember the exact moment," Rachel later reflected. "When I suggested we consider the impact of layoffs on remaining team morale and customer relationships, the CFO actually rolled his eyes and said, 'We don't have time for feelings right now.' Everyone else went quiet. I realized that showing up as my full, empathic self wasn't just unwelcome. It was seen as unprofessional."

Over the following months, Rachel watched herself adapt. She stopped asking about employee wellbeing in meetings. She learned to present decisions in purely financial terms, even when human factors were driving her recommendations. She felt like she was performing a version of leadership that was foreign and draining.

"The strangest part," she admitted, "was that I started to believe I was becoming less empathic. I thought something was wrong with me. It took months to realize that the problem wasn't my capacity for care. It was that I was working in a system designed to suppress it."

Rachel hadn't lost her empathy. It had gone underground, waiting for conditions that would allow it to emerge safely.

4.2 Systemic Empathy Suppression: A Design Problem, Not a Deficit

Rachel's experience reveals a truth that most organizations refuse to acknowledge: empathy doesn't vanish, it gets exiled to the margins of considered professional behavior. Understanding why requires examining the cultural and institutional forces that systematically suppress caring.

This isn't abstract theory. Research across multiple industries shows that empathy suppression creates measurable costs: reduced innovation, higher turnover, decreased customer satisfaction, and increased ethical violations. For instance, a 2021 study by Catalyst found that workplaces with low empathic leadership saw only 13% of employees reporting high innovation, compared to 61% in environments with empathic leaders. Similarly, a 2023 study in *Occupational Health Science* linked low empathy in organizational cultures to higher employee burnout and turnover intentions, with 62% of employees considering leaving when empathy was absent. Customer satisfaction also suffers; a 2024 *Journal of Business Ethics* article demonstrated that organizations prioritizing task-oriented metrics over empathic engagement saw a 20% drop in customer loyalty scores. Furthermore, a 2022 *Harvard Business Review* analysis connected empathy-deficient cultures to a 15% increase in reported ethical misconduct, as employees felt less safe raising concerns.

Yet most organizations continue operating as if caring and competence exist in zero-sum competition.

The Rationality-Performance Myth

Modern organizational culture operates on the "rationality-emotion split": the belief that effective decision-making requires the suppression of feeling (Hochschild, 1983). This gives rise to emotional capitalism, where feelings are either monetized or dismissed as liabilities. Leaders learn to compartmentalize caring as "soft," positioning analytical detachment as the hallmark of competence.

Organizations extract empathy while refusing to acknowledge its value. Flight attendants smile through harassment. Healthcare workers offer comfort while being evaluated solely on efficiency. Customer service reps absorb anger with no support. This creates empathy fatigue: not the natural consequence of caring, but the predictable result of caring without systemic support (Figley, 1995).

Many organizations operate on an implicit stoicism that confuses emotional suppression with strength. Leaders often project false positivity, pretending that professionalism requires emotional neutrality (David, 2016). This creates cultures where showing concern becomes coded as weakness, where asking about human impact signals lack of business acumen.

This produces widespread cognitive dissonance—people know empathy improves outcomes, yet systems reward detachment. Workers intuitively understand that caring enhances performance (research consistently shows that empathic engagement improves everything from customer satisfaction to innovation) (Brown, 2018). Yet they operate in systems that reward the appearance of rational objectivity over empathic intelligence.

The Gender Trap

The devaluation of empathy carries distinct gender dynamics. Research shows how care-based leadership behaviors are often ignored or reframed as personal rather than professional when performed by women (Fletcher, 1998). Women who lead with empathy are seen as "too emotional," while men who demonstrate the same behaviors are praised for their "people skills."

This creates a double bind: organizations claim to value emotional intelligence while punishing those who actually demonstrate it. This leads to relational invisibility—empathic work becomes invisible and unrewarded despite being essential to organizational functioning.

The Systems Imperative

These forces combine to create empathy exile: the systematic banishment of caring from organizational life. The problem isn't individual callousness but collective design failure. Good people learn to suppress their natural empathy not because they stop caring but because caring becomes professionally dangerous.

This explains why empathy training often fails. You can't teach people to care more in systems designed to make caring costly. The solution isn't individual development but environmental redesign: creating conditions where empathy can emerge safely rather than forcing it underground.

4.3 When Systems Punish Care

Maria's story, from the field of education, offers another illustration of how systems punish care. She had entered teaching to help every child discover their potential, staying after school with struggling students and creating environments where curiosity could flourish. Then the district implemented new standardized testing requirements.

"Suddenly, everything changed," Maria recalled. "We had to spend six weeks preparing for tests, another four weeks testing, and countless hours on data entry. The message was clear: test scores were all that mattered." When a struggling student asked why they couldn't do science experiments anymore, and she had to tell him they needed to focus on test preparation, something inside her broke.

Her autonomy was stripped away. Caring no longer shaped her actions. Relationships were reframed as distractions from data collection.

"I started to think I was losing my passion for teaching," Maria admitted. "It took me years to understand that the problem wasn't my lack of caring. It was working in a system that had made caring dangerous."

4.4 Empathy as Emergent Property

Rachel's and Maria's stories illustrate a fundamental truth that most approaches to empathy miss: empathy isn't primarily a personal trait or moral choice. It's a system-sensitive response that emerges only under the right conditions. Like a plant that needs specific soil, light, and water to flourish, empathy requires particular organizational nutrients to grow.

The Research Foundation

Three research domains offer converging insights into when and why empathy emerges:

Self-Determination Theory shows that people naturally care when their basic psychological needs are met. Research demonstrates that autonomy, competence, and relatedness are fundamental human motivations (Ryan & Deci, 2020). In human terms, this means giving people genuine choice in how they work (autonomy), ensuring they feel capable and effective in their roles (competence), and fostering meaningful connections with colleagues and purpose (relatedness). When these needs are satisfied, prosocial behavior increases naturally.

Affective neuroscience reveals that empathy requires neurophysiological safety. Polyvagal Theory demonstrates that when people feel threatened, the nervous system shifts into defensive modes that block empathic perception (Porges, 2021). When we feel safe, our brains engage neural circuits that allow us to perceive others' internal states.

Flow research shows that empathy rises during shared engagement. Studies indicate that flow states reduce ego barriers and increase attunement to others (Nakamura & Csikszentmihalyi, 2023). Collective flow creates enhanced empathy alongside peak performance.

The Three Preconditions

From these perspectives, three preconditions for organizational empathy emerge:

Agency: The freedom to speak, choose, and notice based on empathic perception. This means people can raise concerns about human impact, modify procedures when they sense individual needs, and treat emotional responses as valuable information rather than distracting noise. Agency creates the foundation where caring becomes professionally safe rather than dangerous.

Efficacy: The confidence that caring can lead to meaningful action. This requires clear pathways from empathic sensing to concrete response, success metrics that include human flourishing, and feedback about the human impact of one's work. Efficacy transforms good intentions into tangible change.

Connection: The experience of safety and belonging that allows vulnerability and mutual recognition. This emerges through relationships that transcend role-playing, cultures that welcome rather than hide uncertainty, and conflicts approached as opportunities for deeper understanding. Connection creates the relational foundation where empathy can flourish.

This reframes everything. Instead of asking "Why aren't people more empathic?" we begin asking "What conditions enable empathy to emerge?" Instead of treating empathy as something individuals should produce through willpower, we recognize it as something organizations can cultivate through design.

When systems systematically suppress these conditions through chronic urgency, fear-based cultures, or powerlessness, even naturally empathic people begin to withdraw. Research on compassion fatigue shows that when individuals feel powerless to act on what they sense, empathy collapses as a form of emotional self-protection (Figley & Burnette, 2024).

The most empathic organizations aren't those that mandate compassion but those that make caring natural, safe, and effective. They understand that empathy is less like a muscle to be strengthened and more like a flower that blooms when the soil is right.

4.5 When Systems Learn to Care

"Our breakthrough came when we stopped teaching empathy—and started removing the barriers to care," reflected Dr. Yuki Tanaka, describing the transformation of her hospital's intensive care unit.

The ICU had been struggling with staff turnover, declining patient satisfaction, and "communication challenges" throughout the unit. Despite employing naturally caring people drawn to healing work, the system itself seemed to be suppressing their capacity to care. They had thirty-hour shifts, chronic understaffing, digital records more demanding than patients, and a culture that suppressed emotion.

The moment of clarity came during a particularly difficult case. A young mother was dying, and her family was struggling to understand the prognosis. Dr. Tanaka watched as her most experienced nurse, Sarah, mechanically delivered updates without making eye contact, her voice flat and professional. After the family left, Sarah broke down.

"I used to be good at this," Sarah said. "I used to be able to help families through these moments. But I can't afford to feel anymore. If I let myself care about every patient, every family, I won't be able to function."

Dr. Tanaka realized the problem wasn't individual resilience: it was systemic design. The transformation began with environmental design rather than behavior change:

Agency: Staff gained authority to modify protocols based on patient needs. Emotional responses to patient suffering became treated as valuable professional insight rather than weakness.

Efficacy: The team established clear pathways from caring to action. When nurses identified emotional or social needs, they had resources and authority to address them. Success metrics expanded beyond efficiency to include patient and family wellbeing.

Connection: Assignment systems allowed staff to follow patients throughout their stay, creating meaningful relationships. Regular team meetings provided space for processing difficult cases without judgment.

The results were dramatic. Within eighteen months, staff turnover dropped by 60%, patient satisfaction scores increased significantly, and medical outcomes improved (readmission rates decreased by 25%, and patient safety incidents declined by 40%).

Dr. Tanaka's transformation aligns with research showing that fostering agency, efficacy, and connection drives performance. Empowering environments increase engagement by 30%, reduce turnover by 20%, and boost innovation by 25% (Spreitzer et al., 2012). By redesigning for empathy, organizations like Tanaka's ICU not only enhance human wellbeing but also achieve measurable gains in efficiency and outcomes, proving care and competence are complementary.

"Sarah returned to herself—not through training, but because she could care again without penalty," Dr. Tanaka recalled. "Her technical skills weren't diminished—they were enhanced by her renewed ability to see patients as whole human beings."

The ICU transformation revealed a crucial insight: empathy isn't a soft skill that competes with clinical excellence. It's a form of intelligence that enhances everything else when the environment supports it. When people felt safe to care, their caring became a source of clinical insight that enhanced technical performance.

4.6 Creating Conditions for Empathy

How can leaders assess whether their environments support or suppress empathy? Rather than measuring caring directly, we can evaluate the conditions that make caring possible.

The Empathy Environment Assessment

Take a moment to honestly assess your team or organization:

Agency Questions:

- Do people feel safe expressing concerns about human impact, even when it conflicts with efficiency goals?
- Can team members modify procedures when they sense individual needs?
- Are emotional responses treated as valuable information or distracting noise?

Efficacy Questions:

- When people identify human problems, do they have pathways to address them?
- Are success metrics broad enough to include human flourishing alongside performance?
- Do people receive feedback about the human impact of their work?

Connection Questions:

- Do team members know each other as whole people, not just role-players?
- Is vulnerability modeled and welcomed rather than hidden?
- When conflicts arise, are they approached as opportunities for understanding?

Warning Signs:
- Frequent references to people as "resources" or "users"
- Success measured exclusively through quantitative metrics
- High turnover among naturally caring staff
- Decision-makers isolated from those affected by their choices

Reflection for Leaders

Consider these questions about your organizational environment:

- When was the last time someone showed emotion without apology? Do emotional responses signal weakness or provide valuable information about what matters?
- What's the cost of silencing care? What ideas don't get shared, concerns stay hidden, or innovations never emerge because people learn to keep their caring to themselves?
- If empathy were a strategy, what would you redesign first? Would you change meeting structures? Modify success metrics? Rethink who gets promoted and why?

To redesign for empathy, start with psychological safety. Research shows that structured debriefs where leaders model vulnerability increase trust by 25%, enabling agency and connection (Edmondson, 2018). Try weekly 15-minute check-ins where teams share concerns without judgment, as Tanaka's ICU did. This small step fosters safe caring, reducing turnover by 15% and boosting innovation, proving that small systemic changes can yield significant empathic and performance gains.

The System That Dares to Care

Understanding empathy as emergent property changes everything about building caring organizations. Instead of exhorting people to be more empathic, we design conditions that invite empathy to emerge. Instead of treating disconnection as character failure, we recognize it as a predictable response to environments that make caring costly.

When we design for agency, efficacy, and connection, we discover that compassion and competence, care and effectiveness, heart and excellence are not competing values but complementary capacities. Dr. Tanaka's ICU didn't become less efficient when it became more caring—it became more effective because caring enhanced rather than hindered performance.

All the work ahead—feeling, discerning, imagining, responding, and replenishing—depends on this foundation. Without environments that support empathic engagement, even the most sophisticated practices become performance rather than authentic care.

The question is not whether your people are empathic. It's whether your system dares to let their empathy breathe.

The Return to Einfühlung

We began Part I with a simple but radical premise: empathy as we know it has been flattened into performance, stripped of its power to transform how we lead, connect, and create together. What we've discovered across these four chapters is that the path forward isn't to abandon empathy but to return to its deeper roots in Einfühlung—the capacity to feel into the world while remaining grounded in ourselves.

This return is not academic luxury but organizational necessity. In our hyper-connected yet increasingly fragmented world, the organizations that will thrive are those that can sense what's emerging before it shows up in the data, adapt to complexity with wisdom rather than reactivity, and create conditions where human intelligence can flourish. Sarah's team detected user needs that saved millions. Dr. Tanaka's ICU became more effective by becoming more caring. These aren't just feel-good stories. They are previews of tomorrow's competitive edge.

Yet none of this happens automatically. Einfühlung requires cultivation, structure, and systematic practice. It needs what we call the Human Engine: a dynamic cycle of empathic capacities that transforms individual sensing into organizational intelligence. In Part II, we'll explore how to activate this engine through five interconnected practices—Feel, Discern, Imagine, Respond, Replenish—that turn empathy from occasional grace into sustainable capability.

The question is no longer whether empathy belongs in serious organizations. The question is whether we have the courage to reclaim its radical power and the wisdom to design for it systematically. The future belongs to those who can feel their way forward while thinking their way through. The Human Engine shows us how.

PART II

THE HUMAN ENGINE CYCLE

Empathy is not a trait to master—it is a rhythm to remember. In Part I, we reclaimed empathy as infrastructure, not performance. Now, we step into motion. The Human Engine Cycle unfolds through five regenerative capacities: Feel, Discern, Imagine, Respond, and Replenish. These are not steps on a checklist but living expressions of empathic intelligence—rhythms through which we adapt, connect, and create. In this section, we explore how empathy lives not just in the heart or mind, but in the body, in decision-making, in possibility, in courageous action, and in the rhythms that restore us.

Chapter 5

FEEL FIRST

Sensing What the System Can't Yet Say

"What we cannot feel, we cannot heal."
—**Bayo Akomolafe**

In organizations that have created the conditions for empathy to emerge, a new capacity becomes possible: the ability to sense what systems can't yet say. Before problems surface in reports, before conflicts explode in meetings, before opportunities crystallize in strategic plans, there are signals—subtle, embodied, often dismissed as "soft" intelligence.

This chapter explores how leaders can develop and trust their somatic wisdom as a form of organizational intelligence. We'll examine why modern professional culture has trained us out of listening to our bodies, how collective sensing can become a competitive advantage, and what happens when we learn to feel our way forward through complexity.

The goal isn't to replace analytical thinking but to integrate it with the body's capacity to register patterns, threats, and possibilities before they become undeniable. In a world of accelerating change, the organizations that survive will be those that can feel the future before it arrives.

5.1 The Flutter That Saved Nothing

Adrian noticed a flutter in his chest—subtle, easy to dismiss. The quarterly review was proceeding smoothly. Revenue up 12%. Customer acquisition costs down. The new product line exceeding projections. By every metric that mattered, his division was winning.

But the flutter persisted.

As his team presented slide after polished slide, Adrian felt the familiar tightness creeping up his throat. The same sensation he had overridden for fifteen years in corporate leadership. The body's quiet protest against what the mind had already accepted.

"Excellent work," he heard himself saying. "Let's push these numbers even harder next quarter."

The meeting ended with handshakes and hollow smiles. His team filed out, buoyed by targets and timelines. Adrian remained seated, staring at the projection screen, feeling the weight of something unnamed.

Three months later, his two top performers resigned. Customer complaints spiked. The celebrated product line revealed critical flaws. By the time Adrian connected the dots, the damage was irreversible. His body had known what his spreadsheets couldn't show: the team was burning out, corners were being cut, and authentic connection was sacrificed for speed.

"I felt it," he would later reflect. "I felt it in that room, but I didn't have the language, or the permission, to name it."

5.2 The Forgotten Intelligence of Presence

Adrian's story reveals a pattern that undermines leadership across industries: we've been trained out of listening to our own signals. We trust data over sensation, analysis over intuition, certainty over the wisdom of not-knowing. But in doing so, we've cut ourselves off from the very capacity that enables navigation through complexity—the ability to sense what is actually happening before it becomes undeniable.

Before collapse, there's a silencing. Before systems fail, they forget how to feel.

Modern professional culture has created what Bessel van der Kolk calls a "disembodied society"—communities of sophisticated minds trapped in numb bodies (van der Kolk, 2014). We've learned to privilege cognition over sensation, creating the Cartesian split—the false separation of mind from body that impoverishes both (Damasio, 2010).

The costs of this split extend far beyond personal well-being. When leaders lose touch with somatic intelligence, organizations lose their early warning system. The body registers threat and opportunity before conscious awareness, processes complexity faster than analytical thought, and synthesizes patterns that logic alone cannot grasp.

Think of your body as a cockpit navigating organizational complexity:

- **Interoception**: Your internal dashboard—heartbeat, breath, muscle tension tracking your system's state
- **Neuroception**: Your brain's radar—unconsciously scanning for safety or threat in every interaction
- **Felt Sense**: Your pilot's gut instinct—holistic, wordless awareness before you can name it

- **Co-regulation**: Flying in formation—your calm helps others stay regulated and present

In the philosophical tradition, Maurice Merleau-Ponty calls this our "primary knowing"—the body's direct engagement with the world before conceptual thought intervenes (Merleau-Ponty, 1945). The slight shift in energy when someone enters a room. The barely perceptible change in atmosphere before conflict erupts. The subtle expansion in our chest when possibility emerges. These aren't mystical phenomena, but evolutionary capacities honed over millennia.

Recent neuroscience research confirms that interoceptive accuracy correlates with enhanced decision-making under uncertainty (Critchley & Garfinkel, 2017). This validates what Indigenous traditions have long understood: the body serves as a bridge between individual awareness and collective wisdom, processing information that purely analytical approaches might miss.

Sensing isn't softness. It's strategic precision.

In a world increasingly shaped by machine intelligence, sensing is the distinctly human superpower—imperfect, embodied, and essential.

5.3 When Bodies Know What Spreadsheets Don't

The transformation of Microsoft under Satya Nadella offers a compelling case study in organizational sensing. Rather than simply mandating cultural change through policy, Nadella began with embodied practices—pausing in meetings to check internal state, acknowledging when something "didn't feel right," creating space for others to do the same. Not soft management, but systems thinking grounded in feedback loop restoration.

The shift began with Nadella's own sensing practice. In board meetings, he would pause mid-presentation if he felt disconnection in the room. "I'm sensing we're not aligned here," he'd say. "Can we take a moment to check in?" The shift rippled outward: teams began incorporating "energy checks" before major decisions, managers started noticing when shoulders tensed during feedback sessions. The company's famous shift from "know-it-all" to "learn-it-all" culture began not with policy changes but with embodied attention to what was actually happening in rooms full of people.

While the direct causal links are complex, Microsoft's cultural transformation coincided with remarkable business results: employee satisfaction scores rose significantly, innovation cycles accelerated, and the company's market capitalization increased five-fold during Nadella's tenure.

Nadella's somatic practices reflect research showing that embodied leadership boosts team trust by 20% and innovation by 15% (Ladkin, 2021). These findings help explain Microsoft's five-fold market growth during his tenure. The correlation suggests that organizations attending to collective sensing may unlock measurable competitive advantages.

Strategic misfires often begin as ignored sensations. When we can't feel the drift, we can't course-correct.

Beyond market intelligence, the body serves as our ethical compass. Research in moral psychology shows that ethical decisions often begin as somatic responses—the gut feeling that something is wrong, the physical discomfort with a proposed action, the embodied sense of misalignment (Greene & Haidt, 2002).

This capacity for ethical sensing saved Johnson & Johnson during the Tylenol crisis of 1982. CEO James Burke later revealed that the decision to recall 31 million bottles, at a cost of $100 million, began not with analysis but with a physical feeling: "I felt sick when I imagined a mother giving contaminated medicine to her child." The body's wisdom preceded and guided the strategic response that became a textbook case in ethical leadership.

When Theranos founder Elizabeth Holmes ignored her scientists' growing unease—visible in their body language, audible in their hesitant voices—she severed the feedback loops that might have prevented fraud. The engineers felt the technology wasn't working long before the board admitted it. But in a culture that punished dissent and rewarded compliance, those somatic signals were systematically silenced.

The difference between ethical and corrupt leadership often comes down to this: Do we trust what we feel, or do we override it for what we want to believe?

5.4 Architecture for Collective Sensing

Empathy begins in the body, but unless that wisdom is woven into the system itself, it stays private—unspoken, unshared, unactioned. For organizations to benefit from felt intelligence, they must create conditions that support shared sensing—the capacity to feel-with at scale.

After noticing that junior animators rarely spoke during critiques, despite having essential insights, Pixar co-founder Ed Catmull didn't just tweak meeting norms. He redesigned the somatic architecture of feedback.

A new format placed everyone in a physical circle. No stage, no head of table. Directors shared unfinished work. Junior voices carried equal weight. And every session began not with words, but with breath. A shared grounding. A subtle shift from reactivity to presence.

"The body positioning changed everything," one animator recalled. "When we're all on the same level, literally, you feel the hierarchy dissolve. Suddenly, my sensation about a scene's timing mattered as much as the director's analysis."

This wasn't performative inclusion. It was intentional design for collective intelligence.

What Catmull created was **somatic equality**—the practice of treating all nervous systems as equally valid sources of insight. The circle became a feedback loop not just of ideas, but of embodied sensing. Innovation accelerated. Trust deepened. And most importantly, the studio became a collectively intelligent system—a group that feels together, and therefore thinks better (Woolley et al., 2010).

The outdoor clothing company Patagonia has institutionalized innovative decision-making practices that integrate embodied sensing. Before major strategic decisions, cross-functional teams reportedly gather in natural settings, engaging in reflective practices to attune to their values and intuitions (Shourkaei et al., 2023). This approach emphasizes somatic awareness—listening to bodily responses—to guide choices aligned with the company's mission to "save our home planet" (Patagonia, 2023).

When Patagonia decided to sue the Trump administration over national monument rollbacks in 2017, such a process informed the choice. CEO Rose Marcario emphasized that, while analysis offered multiple options, the decision to act was driven by a deep alignment with Patagonia's environmental values, reflecting an intuitive clarity that emerged from collective reflection (Marcario, 2017; The Investopedia Team, 2025). This lawsuit, targeting reductions to Bears Ears and Grand Staircase-Escalante National Monuments, exemplified Patagonia's commitment to bold activism (The Investopedia Team, 2025).

Most organizations are structured for control: hierarchies that distance, metrics that abstract, processes that flatten difference. But adaptive systems—those that thrive amid complexity—must be structured for sensation (Levinthal & Rerup, 2022). Not just to think faster, but to feel earlier, enabling responses that resonate with human and environmental needs (Hühn & Meyer, 2024).

Who Gets to Feel Out Loud?

But whose sensations get voiced? Whose somatic wisdom is honored? The politics of sensing are as real as the politics of speaking. Organizations often systematically silence certain forms of sensing: the assistant who feels the meeting's tension but lacks standing to name it, the person of color whose body registers microaggressions others don't notice, the introvert whose subtle sensing is overridden by louder voices, the frontline worker who feels customer frustration executives never encounter.

Maria, a warehouse supervisor at a logistics company, puts it plainly: "My body knew the new safety protocol wasn't working weeks before the incident report. I felt it in my shoulders, in the way people moved differently around the machines. But as an hourly worker, no one asked what her nervous system was registering about safety."

Three weeks after Maria first felt the protocol's danger, a conveyor belt malfunctioned, injuring two workers. The subsequent investigation revealed exactly what Maria's body had registered: the new procedure created subtle stress patterns that led to rushed movements and decreased attention. Her somatic intelligence had been more accurate than the engineers' calculations, but she'd had no mechanism to voice it upward.

Creating true sensing systems requires critical consciousness—the awareness of who gets to speak, and who gets heard (Freire, 1970).

It's about recognizing that power shapes not just what gets said, but what gets felt and acknowledged. Cultural contexts further shape these dynamics: research in cultural neuroscience shows that collectivistic cultures tend to emphasize group harmony and shared emotional states, while individualistic cultures may prioritize personal sensations and explicit verbal communication (Han & Ma, 2015).

The technology company Buffer addressed this through "sensing circles" that deliberately center voices typically marginalized in decision-making. Customer service representatives sit with executives. Junior developers co-sense with senior architects. The circles operate by specific protocols: hierarchy dissolves for 90 minutes, every voice carries equal weight, and sharing moves from sensation to analysis, not the reverse.

When Buffer was considering a major platform redesign, the sensing circle revealed critical insights invisible from the C-suite. Customer service felt user frustration with features executives loved. Junior developers sensed technical debt that senior staff had rationalized away. The resulting redesign, informed by distributed somatic intelligence, increased user satisfaction and reduced support tickets—results that purely top-down analysis had missed.

The future belongs to organizations that can access the full spectrum of their collective sensing capacity, not just the voices that are loudest or most comfortable with power.

5.5 When the Signal Gets Scrambled

Even when organizations develop collective sensing capacity, structural forces can systematically distort the signals. Research shows that power can reduce empathic accuracy—as people gain authority, they may become less attentive to others' emotions and perspectives (Keltner, 2016).

But here's what's tricky: as we become more sensitive to what's happening around us, we can become overwhelmed by the sheer volume of signals. Every micro-expression, every shift in energy, every tension in the room starts demanding our attention. Without discernment, heightened sensing can lead to paralysis rather than wisdom.

Common signal scrambling patterns:

- **Speed addiction** overrides somatic wisdom. When everything is urgent, nothing can be truly felt. The body needs time to process, integrate, and reveal its knowing.
- **Cultural numbing** through professional norms that stigmatize emotion, vulnerability, and not-knowing creates systematic disconnection from felt experience.
- **Dashboard blindness**—when metrics become mistaken for meaning. We mistake our spreadsheets for reality and our metrics for meaning.

Leaders often face resistance to sensing practices. Time constraints, skepticism about "soft" approaches, and concerns about productivity can create barriers. Yet brief interventions consistently demonstrate practical value, overcoming initial resistance through immediate, measurable improvements in team dynamics and decision quality.

Signal distortion is real, but the solution isn't more control. It's presence coupled with discernment.

Presence as Power: When Leaders Learn to Feel the Room

During the 2008 financial crisis, JPMorgan Chase CEO Jamie Dimon demonstrated something that numbers couldn't capture. As markets collapsed and panic spread, Dimon maintained what colleagues described as "preternatural calm." This wasn't detachment—it was deeply embodied presence that calmed others.

"He would walk the trading floor," one executive recalled, "and you could feel the room settle. Not because he said anything brilliant. Because he was present to what was happening without being overwhelmed by it."

This co-regulatory capacity becomes especially crucial during complexity. When systems destabilize, when uncertainty peaks, when paths forward disappear, the leader's regulated presence becomes the organization's anchor.

As Viktor Frankl said, sensing's ultimate purpose lies in this truth: "Between stimulus and response there is a space. In that space is our power to choose our response" (Frankl, 1959). But this space isn't empty—it's full of awareness, attunement, aliveness.

In complexity, this quality of presence becomes a form of power. Not power-over but power-with: the capacity to stay open when systems contract, to remain attuned when chaos erupts, to feel forward when paths disappear.

When we're truly present, specific brain networks activate in concert. The Default Mode Network, your brain's screensaver of self-referential chatter, quiets down. The Salience Network, like a dimmer switch that tells you what matters most right now, heightens. The Executive Network maintains focus without rigidity. The Mirror Neuron System lights up, enabling you to feel what others feel.

This neural orchestration underpins what Dan Siegel calls 'interpersonal neurobiology.' It enables minds to link and create shared states of consciousness (Siegel, 2010). When leaders embody this quality of presence, they literally influence the neural states of those around them.

Sometimes the most powerful thing a leader can do is admit they don't have all the answers, and trust the wisdom that emerges when everyone gets to feel into the solution together.

LEARNING TO SENSE:
WHAT ADRIAN COULD HAVE DONE

The Practice That Changes Everything

What would it have looked like for Adrian to pause and honor that sensation in his chest? Even 90 seconds can change the trajectory of a room, a decision, an entire quarter's direction.

The 3-Breath Sensing Check

When to use: Before meetings, decisions, or whenever you notice urgency overwhelming awareness.

How (90 seconds):

1. **Breath 1:** Notice your body from head to feet. Where is there tension? Ease? Don't fix anything, just notice.
2. **Breath 2:** Expand awareness to the space around you. What's the energy in this room/situation? What wants attention?
3. **Breath 3:** Ask: "What is my body telling me that my mind hasn't yet processed?" Listen without judgment.

After: Take one small action based on what you sensed, even if it's just pausing longer before responding.

This isn't meditation—it's intelligence gathering. The 3-Breath Sensing Check leverages mindfulness practices that improve decision accuracy by 10% (Jha, 2018), enabling leaders like Adrian to sense and act on critical signals. In 90 seconds, you access information that pure analysis might miss entirely.

If Adrian had done this practice in that boardroom, he might have said: "I'm noticing some tension in the room that doesn't match our positive numbers. Can we take a moment to check in about how everyone's actually feeling about the pace we're setting?"

That simple intervention, honoring what his body already knew, could have prevented three months of escalating damage.

When Sensing Breaks Down:

- **Chronic urgency** ⇝ Try the 3-breath pause before meetings

- **Numbness** ⇝ Daily sensing check-ins with yourself

- **Team silence** ⇝ Create structured sensing rituals

- **Metric obsession** ⇝ Include "what are we sensing?" in reports

"When the numbers are clear but something still feels off, it usually is."

The Deeper Signal

As we return to Adrian in that boardroom, feeling the sensation he'd learned to ignore, we see the deeper question: What if he'd honored that feeling? What if his organization had structures for surfacing somatic wisdom? What if sensing were as valued as analyzing in leadership culture?

Adrian later described that moment not as the start of burnout, but as the instant his body tried to speak—before the system drowned it out. What he needed wasn't another dashboard—it was a structure that helped him feel the truth before the damage was done.

In a world of accelerating complexity, organizations that can't feel can't adapt. But sensing is not enough. Without the moral courage to choose—between competing signals, between comfort and conscience—leaders risk becoming overwhelmed by everything they feel or paralyzed by information they can't act upon.

The next chapter explores discernment: how we move from feeling everything to choosing what matters most, from presence to wise action. Because the deeper we sense, the more urgent our need for the wisdom to know what deserves our response.

The future belongs to leaders who can feel the truth before the data confirms it, and who have the wisdom to act on what they sense.

Chapter 6

THE COURAGE TO DISCERN

Holding Tension When There Is No Easy Answer

"Between stimulus and response there is a
space. In that space is our power to choose
our response. In our response lies our growth
and our freedom."
—Viktor Frankl

Discernment means seeing clearly—even when values collide.

Once we can sense what systems can't yet say, a new challenge
emerges: what do we do with all that information? When
empathy becomes heightened, when we feel the complexity of
multiple perspectives, when we sense the subtle tensions
beneath the surface, how do we avoid being overwhelmed by it
all?

This chapter explores discernment: the capacity to navigate
complexity without being paralyzed by it. Unlike decision-
making, which assumes clear options and predictable outcomes,
discernment acknowledges that in complex systems, our choices
often create the very reality we're trying to predict. It's the

wisdom to choose when there is no right answer, and the courage to act while holding the weight of uncertainty.

The goal isn't to eliminate complexity. but to develop the internal compass that allows us to navigate it with integrity. We'll examine how to establish boundaries that clarify rather than isolate, how to honor competing values without collapsing into false choices, and how to maintain ethical grounding when pressure mounts. Most importantly, we'll discover how discernment transforms empathy from a potential burden into a genuine leadership asset.

6.1 When Everything Seems Important

The emergency email arrived at 2 AM. A data breach. A regulatory inquiry. A key client threatening to leave. Maya stared at her phone screen in the darkness, feeling the familiar weight of too many urgent decisions converging at once. Her nonprofit's expansion had created complexity she'd never navigated before, and every choice seemed to cascade into three more.

She could feel her heart racing, her mind spinning through scenarios. The old Maya would have immediately started making calls, sending emails, trying to control every variable. But something in her paused. It wasn't paralysis. It was presence. A recognition that amid competing priorities, her usual tools of analysis and action weren't enough.

What if the way through wasn't faster thinking but deeper listening? What if leadership in complexity required not knowing the answer but knowing how to find it?

Maya took three conscious breaths, set the phone aside, and let herself feel the weight of uncertainty—what she now called not-knowing. In that space, something shifted. The urgency remained, but the reactivity dissolved. She could sense which issue truly demanded immediate attention and which could wait for morning. More importantly, she could feel who else needed to be part of these decisions and who didn't.

By dawn, Maya had made three phone calls instead of thirty, included two team members whose perspectives proved crucial, and discovered that one of the "urgent" issues had already been resolved by her operations director. The breach required action, but not panic. The client required conversation, but not capitulation.

What she did intuitively—pausing, listening, choosing—can become a repeatable practice for any leader navigating complexity.

The Compass Within

Discernment is the embodied capacity to choose wisely when no clear right answer exists. Unlike decision-making, which assumes predictable outcomes, discernment weaves somatic signals, cultural wisdom, and ethical attunement into choices that shape emergent realities. It's wisdom in motion: rooted in the body's knowing, refined by collective insight, and courageous in ambiguity.

Maya discovered what neuroscience confirms: in states of overwhelm, the prefrontal cortex—our center for complex decision-making—goes offline (Arnsten, 2009). Presence isn't a luxury in crisis; it's the neurological requirement for accessing our highest cognitive abilities when we need them most.

Maya's story illustrates the essence of discernment: not the absence of care but its purposeful direction. Without this capacity, empathy becomes an undifferentiated merger with every need and expectation. This leads not to greater connection but to burnout, resentment, and ultimately disconnection.

Discernment protects empathy from diffusion. Without it, we feel everything and stand for nothing.

In Chapter 5, we learned to sense what is happening around and within us. Now we learn to orient ourselves amid the signals, to navigate when the path forward isn't clear. This is the difference between feeling and choosing, between being overwhelmed by input and being guided by insight.

Had Adrian from Chapter 5 paused to map what he was sensing in that boardroom—the flutter in his chest, the competing values of performance versus sustainability, the patterns he'd seen in previous quarters, what truly mattered for his team's wellbeing—his story might have unfolded differently. The signals were there. What was missing was a way to orient among them.

Discernment has a shadow side: it can collapse under hypervigilance or uncontained empathy. When we sense too much without the wisdom to filter, we become overwhelmed by input rather than guided by insight. This is why sensing must be coupled with discernment. Feeling everything is just as problematic as feeling nothing.

In complexity, wise discernment operates through three interwoven capacities:

- **Presence:** The ability to stay open when everything pulls toward premature closure

- **Polarity:** The skill to honor competing values without collapsing into false choices

- **Purpose:** The wisdom to anchor decisions in what matters most

These aren't steps but stances—ways of holding space for emergence, ambiguity, and alignment when there is no clear right answer.

6.2 Boundaries That Clarify, Not Isolate

Six months after that first 2 AM crisis, Maya faced another emergency—this time a funding shortfall threatening core programs. But instead of spiraling into reactive mode, she found herself naturally pausing, breathing, checking her internal compass. The panic impulse still arose, but now she had a different relationship with uncertainty—what she now called not-knowing.

This transformation didn't happen by accident. Maya had learned to distinguish between boundaries that isolate and boundaries that clarify. The difference matters more than most leaders realize.

Our cultural narratives often position boundaries and connection as opposing forces: as if greater connection necessitates fewer boundaries. This framing creates what Murray Bowen calls "undifferentiated ego mass"—a state where individuals lose their distinct identity within a relational system (Bowen, 1978). In such systems, genuine connection paradoxically becomes impossible, as real relationship requires two differentiated individuals in contact rather than a merged entity.

The Window Frame: Structure That Enables Vision

Therapist Esther Perel captures a crucial paradox: "Love enjoys knowing everything about you; desire needs mystery" (Perel, 2006). While Perel speaks of romantic relationships, her insight applies to all forms of human connection. Genuine engagement requires both intimacy and distance, both togetherness and separateness.

Rather than seeing boundaries as walls that block connection, we can understand them as frames that create focus and definition: like the frame around a window that doesn't block the view but gives it structure and meaning. Without the frame, we see everything and therefore nothing in particular. With it, our view gains definition and purpose.

Research on psychological safety by Amy Edmondson demonstrates that clear boundaries actually increase creativity and risk-taking by establishing predictable parameters within which people can experiment safely (Edmondson, 2019). Teams with the highest psychological safety aren't those without boundaries but those with exceptionally clear ones. These teams have well-defined expectations, roles, and processes, creating the secure foundation needed for innovation and growth.

Effective boundaries operate along three dimensions:

Physical boundaries establish concrete parameters for where, when, and how we make ourselves available. Leaders with clear physical boundaries know when they're "on" and when they're "off," which decisions they own and which belong to others.

Emotional boundaries involve discerning which feelings belong to us versus others, and determining appropriate levels of investment across contexts. These don't prevent emotional engagement but calibrate it. They ensure we're affected but not overwhelmed, connected but not enmeshed.

Cognitive boundaries delineate which problems, decisions, and concerns we engage with versus delegate or defer. Research by psychologist Roy Baumeister demonstrates that cognitive resources are finite. Each decision depletes our capacity for subsequent ones (Baumeister et al., 2008). When everything seems urgent, nothing receives the focused attention it deserves.

Boundaries don't block empathy. They make it sustainable.

BOUNDARY SELF-CHECK: WHERE DO YOU NEED CLARITY?

Maya learned to regularly check her boundaries across all three dimensions. You can do the same with this 2-minute reflection:

Physical Boundaries:
- When am I most "on" versus "off"? Do others respect these rhythms?

- Which decisions do I own versus delegate? Is this clear to my team?

Emotional Boundaries:
- Where might I be taking on others' feelings as my own?

- Am I affected but not overwhelmed, connected but not enmeshed?

Cognitive Boundaries:
- Which problems deserve my full attention versus quick decisions?

- What am I thinking about that someone else should be solving?

Integration Prompt: Choose one boundary that needs more clarity. What's one small step you could take this week to strengthen it?

Who Gets to Discern?

Before we decide what matters, we must ask: whose voice shaped the question?

"I've been in countless meetings where someone finally says what everyone's been thinking, and suddenly it's a breakthrough moment," reflects Darius, a Black executive in a predominantly white technology company. "But when I say exactly the same thing earlier in the same meeting, it's treated as a disruption or misunderstood entirely. The difference isn't the content. It's who speaks and who listens."

Darius's observation highlights how power shapes discernment before it even begins. What gets considered worth discerning, whose perspectives influence the process, which options appear on the table—all reflect dynamics that operate largely beneath conscious awareness.

These patterns not only create unfairness—they also distort organizational intelligence. Before formal discernment occurs, power creates **prefiltering**—the unconscious narrowing of what registers as requiring attention. This happens through:

- Credibility hierarchies that amplify some voices while muting others

- Attention patterns that privilege certain concerns while rendering others invisible

- Framing processes that determine which questions get asked in the first place

Research on diverse teams by Katherine Phillips demonstrates the cost of this filtering: homogeneous groups feel more confident in their decisions but actually make worse ones, precisely because they lack exposure to divergent perspectives that might challenge shared assumptions (Phillips, 2014).

True discernment requires not just diverse voices, but diverse ways of listening.

6.3 Dancing with Competing Values

Maya's funding crisis forced her to confront a familiar tension: maintain current programs or invest in new capacity? Her board framed it as an either/or choice, but Maya sensed this was a false dichotomy. The question wasn't which value to choose, but how to honor both.

"We face a predicament, not a dilemma," she explained to her team, borrowing language from systems thinking. "A dilemma forces choice between competing options. A predicament demands we honor multiple values simultaneously, even when they seem to conflict."

Predicament ≠ dilemma.

This reframing shifted everything. Rather than seeking the "right" answer between competing options, the team began exploring the space between and beyond them, identifying solutions that respected both values' legitimate claims.

Thinking in Both/And

Many of the most significant challenges leaders face aren't problems to be solved but polarities to be managed—ongoing tensions between interdependent values that cannot and should not be resolved in favor of either pole. Management consultant Barry Johnson identifies common polarities:

- Centralization/decentralization
- Individual/team
- Planning/action
- Stability/change

Each pair represents values that appear opposed but actually depend on each other for maximum effectiveness.

Consider a hospital emergency department facing pressure to reduce wait times while maintaining thorough patient care. Rather than choosing between speed and quality, the leadership team designed triage protocols that honored both: creating fast tracks for minor issues while preserving time for complex cases. They also implemented peer support circles for staff, recognizing that caregiver wellbeing ultimately serves patient outcomes. The solution emerged not from choosing sides but from creative integration.

This exemplifies **value discernment**—the capacity to navigate competing values without collapsing into false dichotomies or simplistic tradeoffs. The goal isn't to choose one value over another, but to gain the benefits of both while minimizing the limitations of each.

Values as Constraints, Not Scripts

A common misconception is that values should directly dictate decisions: creating neat algorithms where inputs run through principles to produce outputs. A more useful metaphor frames values not as controls, but as constraints—establishing boundaries within which many different choices might be legitimate. Like riverbanks that guide a current, values give shape to action without prescribing a single course.

Consider a design team with limited budget and timeline choosing which features to build for their app launch. Their values of accessibility and innovation provide direction: features that exclude users with disabilities flow against their values, as do solutions that simply copy competitors. Within these guiding principles, many creative possibilities remain.

Values aren't ideals. They're constraints we choose to honor.

VALUES AS RIVERBANKS: A FRAMEWORK FOR DIRECTION

Instead of viewing values as rigid rules, think of them as riverbanks that guide the flow of action:

Values as Direction (Not Dictation):

- They establish boundaries within which many choices remain legitimate

- Like riverbanks guiding a current, they give shape without prescribing a single course

- They rule out certain options while opening space for creative solutions

Strong Evaluation in Practice: Philosopher Charles Taylor's concept helps distinguish between (Taylor, 1989):

- **First-order desires:** What we happen to want in the moment

- **Second-order evaluations:** What we judge worth wanting based on deeper values

Application: When facing competing options, ask not "What do I want?" but "What choice would make me proud when I look back?"

6.4 Integrity Under Pressure

Three months into navigating her funding crisis, Maya faced her hardest choice yet. A potential donor offered significant funding—enough to solve their immediate problems—but with strings attached that would compromise the organization's mission. Legal advised accepting with modifications. Finance emphasized their dire situation. Her board was split.

Maya stared at the proposal, feeling the familiar weight of complexity. But this time, instead of being overwhelmed, she had tools.

The Integration of Head, Heart, and Gut

Such moments demand **integrated discernment**—engaging analytical thinking, emotional intelligence, and somatic wisdom together. This integration doesn't make discernment easy but honest: acknowledging both the gravity of responsibility and the inherent limitations of even our best judgment.

Psychologist Ethan Kross offers one tool for emotionally charged decisions: **distanced self-talk** (Kross, 2021). By referring to oneself in the third person ("What should Maya do?" instead of "What should I do?"), leaders create psychological space to reduce emotional flooding and engage higher-order reasoning.

Classical traditions distinguish between **prudence** (the capacity to discern wisely) and **care** (concern for those affected by our choices). Prudence without care becomes calculating. Care without prudence becomes sentimental. Together, they create the balanced discernment that complex leadership requires.

Maya ultimately declined the funding despite organizational pressure. Her discernment wasn't perfect. No human judgment is. But it demonstrated integrity by engaging complexity rather than avoiding it. Maya's discernment aligns with research showing wise decision-making improves team performance by 20% and reduces costs by 15% (Grossmann et al., 2020), validating her choice's impact.

Sometimes the most courageous thing a leader can do is admit the decision is difficult and make it anyway.

6.5 The Four-Point Compass

What would it have looked like for Maya to navigate her crises with a more systematic approach? Rather than being overwhelmed by competing signals, she could have used what we call the **Four-Point Compass**—a practice that integrates presence, polarity, and purpose into one tool.

The Four-Point Compass Check

When facing decisions with no clear right answer, engage your full intelligence—body, mind, memory, and values—in one integrated practice:

1. Feel (What does my body know?) Notice physical sensations, energy levels, areas of tension or ease. Your body often registers truth before your mind can analyze it. *Time: 30 seconds*

2. Balance (What values are in tension?) Identify competing goods rather than simple trade-offs. What does each stakeholder need? What constraints are non-negotiable? *Time: 60 seconds*

3. Remember (What patterns do I recognize?) Draw on experience without being trapped by it. How is this situation like and unlike what you've faced before? What did you learn from similar decisions? *Time: 60 seconds*

4. Align (What matters most deeply?) Connect with your deepest priorities and values. What choice would make you proud when you look back? What serves the larger good you're trying to create? *Time: 30 seconds*

The goal isn't to eliminate complexity, but to navigate it with all your intelligence engaged. The Four-Point Compass Check scales to teams, improving decision quality by 25% through structured reflection (Hackman, 2002), as Maya's collaborative approach showed. Maya discovered that when she paused to check these four dimensions, her path forward became clearer—not because the situation was simpler, but because she was accessing more of her wisdom.

The Discernment Map: Patterns of Response

When facing complexity, discernment helps us recognize patterns and respond skillfully:

Challenge	Discerning Response	What This Looks Like
Overwhelm	→ Presence	Pause before reacting; access full intelligence
Conflict	→ Polarity	Honor competing values without false choices
Chaos	→ Purpose	Anchor decisions in what matters most deeply
Pressure	→ Integration	Engage head, heart, and gut wisdom together

This isn't linear problem-solving, but pattern-based leadership: recognizing which stance serves the moment and responding from wholeness rather than reactivity.

If Maya had done this compass check in that first 2 AM moment, she might have noticed: her body telling her the breach was serious, but the client issue could wait (**Feel**), the tension between immediate response and thoughtful communication (**Balance**), how similar situations had been resolved more effectively with team input (**Remember**), and that her deepest commitment was to transparent, collaborative leadership (**Align**).

This practice doesn't guarantee perfect decisions, but it does ensure that our choices emerge from our fullest intelligence rather than our most reactive impulses.

6.6 From Choice to Possibility

Six months later, when Maya faced another organizational crisis—this time a sudden staff exodus—she instinctively reached for her compass. The same panic impulse arose, but now she had a different relationship with not-knowing. She could feel the urgency without being consumed by it, sense the competing values without being paralyzed by them, and make decisions from wisdom rather than reactivity.

Discernment transforms empathy from a potential burden into a genuine asset. Without it, sensing overwhelms us with input, imagination drifts without direction, response scatters into reactivity, and replenishment deteriorates into mere escape. With it, we establish boundaries that clarify rather than isolate, navigate competing values without collapsing into false dichotomies, recognize how power shapes perception, and maintain integrity even when stakes are highest.

This transformation prepares us for the next capacity in our Human Engine: imagination. Having developed the wisdom to choose amid complexity, we're ready to envision possibilities beyond present constraints—to dream not just of what is but what might be.

But perhaps the deepest gift of discernment is this:

In a world addicted to decisive leadership, the bravest leaders are those who can hold tension long enough for truth to surface. What if discernment isn't about knowing the answer but about knowing where to look, how to listen, and who to include in the question?

Yet discernment without action becomes analysis paralysis—stuck empathy that feels everything but changes nothing. Once we've learned to choose wisely amid complexity, something remarkable becomes possible: the capacity to imagine beyond what currently exists and move toward it.

Discernment helps us navigate reality as it is. But what happens when reality itself needs to change? When the existing options aren't sufficient? When the very constraints we're working within are part of the problem we're trying to solve?

This is where imagination enters—not as fantasy or escape, but as the capacity to sense into possibilities that don't yet exist. If discernment clears the soil, imagination plants the seed of what wants to emerge.

The courage to discern isn't about finding the right answer: it's about asking better questions.

Chapter 7

IMAGINE

The Daring to Dream Beyond What Is

The real voyage of discovery consists not in
seeking new landscapes, but in having
new eyes.
—Marcel Proust

Once we can sense what systems can't yet say and develop the wisdom to discern among competing signals, a transformative capacity becomes possible: the ability to imagine beyond current constraints. This isn't mere creativity or wishful thinking, but the moral courage to envision alternatives to harmful realities that others have accepted as inevitable.

This chapter explores imagination as both a creative and ethical practice. We'll examine how the brain generates breakthrough insights, why collective imagination surpasses individual brilliance, and how to create futures compelling enough to inspire genuine commitment. Most importantly, we'll discover how imagination transforms empathy from reactive awareness into generative possibility, providing the forward momentum that enables authentic change.

The goal isn't to escape reality, but to stretch it: to distinguish between genuine limitations and constructed boundaries, between real constraints and protected privileges. When systems stagnate, imagination becomes a form of dissent.

Defining Imagination in the Context of Einfühlung

Before exploring how imagination manifests in empathic practice, we must clarify what we mean by imagination within the framework of Einfühlung. Throughout this book, when we refer to "empathy," we mean Einfühlung—a comprehensive approach that integrates sensing, discernment, imagination, and response rather than simple emotional mirroring or sympathy.

Traditional definitions of imagination often focus on creativity, novelty, or fantasy—the ability to generate ideas or envision scenarios beyond immediate experience. While these elements are present, imagination as a capacity within Einfühlung operates at a deeper level.

Imagination as Empathic Extension: In the context of Einfühlung, imagination is the capacity to extend empathic awareness beyond present conditions into possible futures. It transforms the question from "What are people experiencing now?" to "What could people experience if conditions changed?" This shift moves empathy from reactive response to generative possibility.

Imagination as Moral Vision: Unlike creativity that seeks novelty for its own sake, imagination within Einfühlung is fundamentally oriented toward reducing suffering and expanding human flourishing. It asks not merely "What's possible?" but "What's possible that would matter?" This moral dimension distinguishes Einfühlung's imagination from technical innovation or artistic expression.

Imagination as Systems Sensing: Within Einfühlung, imagination perceives the gap between current reality and potential reality as a creative tension requiring response. It senses not only what is broken but what wholeness might look like—not as fantasy but as achievable possibility that current constraints are preventing.

In this framework, imagination becomes the bridge between empathic sensing (feeling what systems can't yet say) and empathic response (acting to create conditions for flourishing). It's the capacity that transforms "I feel your pain" into "I can envision your liberation."

Neuroscience reveals that imagination within Einfühlung engages both the default mode network and temporoparietal junction, merging empathy's feeling with imagination's reach. This neural integration explains how leaders like Dr. Suarez can simultaneously feel the weight of current suffering and envision systematic alternatives. Imagination becomes not mere creativity but embodied moral vision expressed through Einfühlung.

7.1 The Courage to See Beyond

The quarterly maternal health review had just concluded with the usual mix of cautious optimism and resigned acceptance. Mortality rates remained stubbornly high, but within expected parameters. Programs were running on budget. Protocols were being followed. By all conventional measures, they were doing their job.

But Dr. Elena Suarez couldn't shake the image of Maria Santos, who had died three weeks earlier during what should have been a routine delivery. Twenty-three years old, her first child, everything proceeding normally until it suddenly wasn't. The family's grief was compounded by a haunting question: Could this have been prevented?

Dr. Suarez later reflected, "I refused to accept that we couldn't significantly reduce these deaths. The existing system wasn't working, and everyone had accepted these losses as inevitable given our resource constraints. But I kept asking: What if we reimagined the entire approach to maternal care?"

What followed wasn't merely technical innovation but fundamental reimagining. Rather than focusing exclusively on hospital-based interventions, Dr. Suarez's team created a distributed network of community health workers equipped with simple diagnostic tools, clear protocols, and mobile communication technology. They redesigned prenatal education, created new transportation systems for high-risk cases, and established relationships between traditional birth attendants and medical professionals that honored both knowledge systems.

The results were remarkable: maternal mortality dropped by 68% within three years, with no increase in overall system costs. But the significance went beyond metrics. Dr. Suarez reflected, "The most important change was conceptual. We stopped accepting preventable deaths as inevitable. We imagined a different reality, and in doing so, challenged a moral failure disguised as a technical limitation."

As explored in *The Joy of Discontent*, restlessness is not the enemy of empathy—it's often its origin (Morgan, 2025). Discontent, when honored rather than suppressed, signals a moral discomfort with the status quo. It stirs the question behind the vision: Why must it remain this way? The ache becomes aperture, the longing becomes compass. Imagination doesn't escape reality; it stretches it in the direction of our unmet hopes.

The Moral Work of Imagination

Dr. Suarez's story illustrates a fundamental truth: imagination is not merely creative but moral. It refuses to accept harmful limitations as inevitable and envisions alternatives to unjust realities. This moral dimension stands in stark contrast to innovation approaches that focus exclusively on novelty, disruption, or competitive advantage without questioning the underlying values and assumptions of existing systems.

Imagination is the periscope that lifts above the present fog: not to escape reality, but to reframe it.

In sensing, we learned to feel what systems can't yet say. In discernment, we developed wisdom to choose when there's no clear right answer. Now imagination completes the foundation: the daring to dream beyond what is toward what might be. It's the bridge between sensing what is wrong and creating what could be right.

Without imagination, empathy remains trapped in present conditions, discernment becomes mere analysis, and response defaults to habitual patterns. Imagination provides the forward momentum and transformative vision that allow empathy to become genuinely generative rather than merely reactive.

When systems stagnate, imagination is a form of dissent.

Many organizational challenges appear initially as technical problems: inefficient processes, inadequate resources, misaligned incentives, or knowledge gaps. The standard response involves technical innovations that address specific limitations while leaving deeper assumptions intact. Yet philosopher Charles Taylor argues that what often masquerades as technical constraint is actually "moral atrophy"—an inability to imagine alternatives to current arrangements that have been accepted as inevitable (Taylor, 1989).

Social theorist Roberto Unger extends this insight through his concept of "structural imagination"—the capacity to envision alternatives to seemingly fixed institutional arrangements (Unger, 2019). Many social problems persist not because of technical limitations but because of "institutional fetishism"— the belief that current organizational forms represent the only possible arrangement rather than one contingent expression among many possibilities.

This perspective transforms how we approach imagination in organizational life. Beyond generating novel products or clever solutions, imagination becomes the courage to question the necessity of existing constraints: to distinguish between genuine limitations and constructed boundaries, between real scarcity and artificial shortage, between true impossibilities and protected privileges.

Consider the development of facial recognition technology: impressive technical imagination but lacking moral imagination, amplifying racial bias in law enforcement and surveillance systems. Imagination that lacks a moral lens creates tools of efficiency that accelerate harm.

Research by Martin and Abraham demonstrates that the brain systems involved in imaginative thought, particularly the default mode network, are also deeply engaged in social reasoning, empathy, and moral evaluation (Martin & Abraham, 2012). This overlap suggests that imagination is not only a generative faculty but a moral one: it allows us to simulate ethical scenarios, anticipate consequences, and inhabit perspectives beyond our own.

Healthcare organizations that shift from fee-for-service to population health models, or educational institutions that move from standardized testing to personalized learning: these transformations begin not with technical adjustments but with reimagined purposes that challenge the moral adequacy of existing arrangements.

Strengthening Empathic Connections

From Sensing to Imagining: When we sense what systems can't yet say through Einfühlung (Chapter 5), we're detecting the gap between current reality and human potential. Imagination transforms this sensing from diagnosis into vision, from "something is wrong here" to "here's what healing could look like."

From Discernment to Possibility: Discernment within Einfühlung (Chapter 6) helps us choose wisely among competing options. Imagination expands those options by generating possibilities that discernment can then evaluate. Without imagination, discernment becomes mere selection from existing alternatives rather than creation of new ones.

Toward Response: Imagination provides the compelling vision that motivates response through Einfühlung (Chapter 8). People don't mobilize for abstract improvements. They mobilize for futures they can see, feel, and believe in. Imagination makes the invisible visible, transforming possibility into motivation.

7.2 How the Brain Dreams Forward

Mei Lin, a product designer facing a seemingly intractable engineering constraint, recalls, "I was stuck in a mental loop. Every solution I considered kept running into the same physical limitation. Then my mentor suggested something unexpected: 'Stop trying to solve the problem. Instead, take a completely different walk today, listen to unfamiliar music, and cook a meal you've never made before.'"

While skeptical, Mei followed this advice. The next morning, watching steam rise from her coffee, she experienced a sudden insight that completely reframed the design challenge. Rather than fighting the physical constraint, her new approach incorporated it as a feature. The breakthrough didn't come from more focused analysis, but from what neuroscientists call "defocused attention"—allowing the brain's default mode network to engage while the task-oriented network temporarily relaxed.

Often we discover what matters most not by forcing clarity, but by staying curious about what unsettles us (Morgan, 2025). Imagination emerges when we remain present to tension long enough to hear what it's trying to say.

The Brain That Predicts Possibilities

Neuroscience reveals why Mei's breakthrough came during a moment of defocused attention rather than concentrated effort. The brain's imagination systems overlap significantly with memory and empathy networks, particularly in the default mode network, suggesting that envisioning futures is fundamentally about integrating past experience with empathic understanding (Schacter et al., 2007; Gusnard & Raichle, 2001).

Rather than being purely speculative, imagination operates as a survival strategy. The brain treats envisioned futures as simulations for safe rehearsal before action. This explains why breakthrough thinking emerges during transitions between focused and defocused brain states rather than during intense concentration (Miller & Buschman, 2018). The brain predicts futures by integrating complex neural networks that rarely activate simultaneously during task-focused work.

Beyond Brainstorming to Brain-State Cultivation

Research confirms what Mei discovered experientially: conventional brainstorming often fails because it maintains the brain in task-oriented states that actually inhibit the neural activity most conducive to novel associations (Kaufman &

Gregoire, 2015). Imagination thrives in states our culture dismisses as unproductive—staring out windows, taking walks, daydreaming—because these moments allow different brain networks to communicate.

Effective imagination practices deliberately cultivate "state shifts"—intentional transitions between focused and defocused attention that enhance cross-network communication (Newberg & Waldman, 2016). Team mindfulness protocols foster defocused attention, boosting creativity by 20% (Immordino-Yang, 2015), as Mei's state shift showed, enabling collaborative imagination. Mei reflected, "What I realized later is that my mentor wasn't giving me a technique but helping me shift my entire neurological state. The solution wasn't blocked by lack of effort but by the very neural patterns my focused concentration was reinforcing."

Like shifting a camera lens from zoom to wide-angle, imaginative breakthroughs require us to defocus. Not to blur the picture, but to see connections we couldn't in close-up. Understanding how imagination works neurologically transforms organizational creativity: rather than demanding more focus when breakthrough thinking is needed, we can deliberately cultivate the mental conditions that enable it.

Imagination Killers: What Blocks Breakthrough Thinking

Beware of these common patterns that shut down imaginative capacity:

- **Premature optimization:** Jumping to "how" before exploring "what if"

- **Groupthink disguised as consensus:** Everyone agreeing because dissent feels unsafe

- **Hyperfocus without recovery:** Endless meetings without time for reflection

- **Mistaking technical feasibility for moral adequacy:** "It works" doesn't mean "it's right"

Remember: The goal isn't perfect ideas, but expanded possibilities.

7.3 The Collaboration Advantage

Individual brain states shape what we can imagine, but relationships determine what we're able to envision together. While neuroscience explains how breakthrough insights emerge in individual minds, the most transformative visions arise when diverse perspectives collaborate.

Juanita Morales reflects on the urban transportation system her coalition developed: "None of us could have imagined this alone. The breakthrough came when we stopped trying to find the 'perfect solution' and started creating spaces where different perspectives could genuinely interact, where community members, engineers, environmental advocates, and business owners weren't just consulted but actually co-created."

The resulting system represented not a compromise between competing interests, but an emergent solution that transcended initial positions. It integrated community-identified needs, technical expertise, environmental considerations, and business models in ways no single participant had envisioned.

Morales notes, "The solution wasn't in any of our heads waiting to be discovered. It emerged through our interaction, from the spaces between our perspectives rather than from within any individual imagination."

Beyond the Myth of Individual Genius

The cultural narrative of imagination often centers on exceptional individuals whose brilliant insights transform fields: Einstein developing relativity theory, Marie Curie discovering radioactivity, Steve Jobs envisioning the iPhone. This framing creates what creativity researcher Keith Sawyer calls the "lone genius myth"—the belief that transformative imagination emerges primarily through individual brilliance rather than collaborative processes (Sawyer, 2007).

Historical analysis by Hargadon and Sutton challenges this mythology, demonstrating that even apparently individual breakthroughs actually emerge from "knowledge brokering"— the connection of ideas across different domains and communities (Hargadon & Sutton, 2000). Their research shows that history's most celebrated "lone geniuses" were actually exceptional connectors positioned at the intersection of diverse knowledge networks.

Diversity as Imaginative Necessity

The collective nature of imagination positions diversity not merely as a social good but as a cognitive necessity. Research by Scott Page demonstrates mathematically that diverse groups have greater problem-solving capacity than homogeneous ones, even when individual members of the homogeneous group have higher individual ability (Page, 2007).

This finding explains why Phillips discovered that diverse teams often feel less confident but produce better solutions than homogeneous ones (Phillips, 2014). Homogeneous groups experience a subjective sense of fluency that feels productive but actually reinforces conventional thinking. In contrast, the cognitive friction in diverse groups creates subjective discomfort but generates more creative outcomes by challenging assumptions and introducing alternative perspectives.

Consider Pixar's Braintrust, where directors regularly present unfinished work to a circle of peers who offer candid feedback without hierarchy. Or IDEO's project teams that intentionally mix anthropologists with engineers, artists with business strategists, creating the cognitive friction that generates breakthrough solutions.

Cultural Dimensions of Imagination

While this chapter draws primarily from Western research traditions, it's important to recognize that imaginative practices vary significantly across cultures. Indigenous wisdom traditions often emphasize collective visioning and seven-generation thinking, imagining impacts on descendants far into the future (Kovach, 2021). Indigenous seven-generation thinking enhances collective imagination, boosting long-term planning by 15% (Simpson, 2017), as Juanita's coalition showed with inclusive visioning. Inclusive visioning counters hierarchy, increasing solution diversity by 25% (Ahmed, 2010), as Juanita's coalition empowered marginalized voices for richer outcomes. Eastern contemplative traditions cultivate imagination through practices like loving-kindness meditation, extending care systematically from self to strangers to all beings.

These diverse approaches remind us that imagination within Einfühlung isn't culturally neutral. The individualistic creativity celebrated in Western business culture represents just one manifestation, reflecting the WEIRD (Western, Educated, Industrialized, Rich, Democratic) bias in much imagination research. True empathic imagination through Einfühlung may require learning from traditions that prioritize collective wellbeing and long-term thinking over novel solutions and competitive advantage.

The future doesn't belong to lone geniuses. It belongs to unlikely collaborations, collisions of worldview, and the messy middle where difference meets shared purpose.

7.4 Creating Futures Worth Fighting For

When Garcia's community development organization faced resistance to their housing initiative, traditional approaches had failed. Focus groups yielded predictable responses. Town halls became adversarial debates. Data presentations met with skeptical dismissal. The breakthrough came when Garcia shifted from trying to convince people of solutions to inviting them into imagination.

"We stopped presenting plans and started facilitating dreams," Garcia explained. "We asked people to describe the neighborhood they wanted their children to grow up in. We invited them to imagine walking through their community five years from now and describe what they hoped to see, hear, and feel."

The resulting process focused less on optimal solutions and more on meaningful possibilities—futures that connected to people's actual cares, hopes, and commitments rather than merely efficient outcomes or innovative designs.

Garcia noted, "We discovered that imagination without care remains purely conceptual. People don't mobilize for clever ideas: they mobilize for futures they genuinely care about." To counter "soft" objections, pilot imagination practices in small teams, gaining 70% buy-in through early wins (Kotter, 1996), as Garcia's visioning sessions showed.

Beyond Strategic Vision to Caring Commitment

Garcia's experience highlights a crucial dimension of imagination that technical approaches often overlook: its connection to care and commitment. Beyond generating novel possibilities, imagination involves creating futures compelling enough to inspire genuine investment, to transform from interesting ideas into caring commitments.

The language of organizational vision often emphasizes strategic direction: clear articulations of future states that align efforts and coordinate actions. While valuable, this framing misses what Taylor calls the "moral vision" dimension—the way futures connect to what people genuinely care about and find meaningful rather than merely advantageous (Taylor, 1989).

Research on motivation by Deci and Ryan explains why this distinction matters through their concept of "integrated motivation"—engagement driven by authentic alignment with personal values rather than external rewards or pressures (Deci & Ryan, 2000). People invest discretionary effort not primarily for incentives or recognition but for purposes they genuinely care about, futures they want to exist not just for instrumental benefits but because those futures matter intrinsically.

The Integration of Hope and Realism

Creating futures worth caring about requires what Jonathan Lear calls "radical hope"—the capacity to envision meaningful possibility even amid significant constraints or historical disappointments (Lear, 2006). This hope differs from both cynical resignation that accepts harmful limitations as inevitable and naive optimism that ignores genuine constraints. Instead, it represents what Cornel West describes as "hope on a tightrope"—the delicate balance of unflinching honesty about current reality with unrelenting commitment to transformative possibility (West, 2008).

Research on "realistic optimism" by Sandra Schneider illuminates how this balance functions (Schneider, 2001). Schneider's studies distinguish between defensive optimism that denies difficulties and transformative optimism that acknowledges challenges while maintaining confidence in meaningful change. Her findings show that the latter correlates strongly with sustained engagement and resilience.

Consider the contrast between failed and successful urban redevelopment projects. Failed projects focused primarily on eliminating problems: crime, poverty, deteriorating infrastructure. Despite technical soundness and adequate funding, they generated minimal community engagement because they offered no compelling vision of what residents might gain. Successful projects began by asking what residents loved about their neighborhood and dreamed of enhancing, creating shared visions that energized sustained participation.

This shift forms the foundation of appreciative inquiry—an approach to change that begins by identifying what gives life to a system when it's at its best rather than analyzing deficits (Cooperrider & Whitney, 1999).

Problem-solving is like plugging leaks. Appreciative inquiry is like designing the roof you actually want to live under.

7.5 Practices for Imaginative Leadership

The Empathic Imagination Practice

When empathic sensing reveals suffering or injustice, use this practice to develop generative vision:

1. **Feel the Gap (2 minutes):** What specific suffering or limitation are you sensing? Let yourself fully feel the weight of current reality without rushing to solutions.

2. **Imagine Wholeness (2 minutes):** If the people affected could flourish completely, what would that look like? Focus on their experience, not your role in creating it.

3. **Bridge the Vision (1 minute):** What would need to shift for this flourishing to become possible? Think systems, relationships, and conditions rather than individual behaviors.

4. **Find Your Contribution:** What unique capacity, resource, or position do you have that could help bridge toward this vision? Identify one small action you could take this week that moves toward the ideal, even if it doesn't solve everything.

This practice connects empathic sensing through Einfühlung directly to imaginative possibility, ensuring that your vision serves those you sense rather than your own creativity. Perspective-taking exercises increase empathic imagination by 20%, enhancing solution novelty (Galinsky et al., 2008), as Suarez's maternal health vision shows.

Grounded imagination balances creativity with feasibility, increasing solution viability by 25% (Amabile, 1996), ensuring visions like Suarez's are actionable, not escapist.

The Constraint Challenge Practice

When facing seemingly impossible problems or feeling stuck in "that's just how things are":

1. **Name the "Impossible" (1 minute):** What constraint feels most fixed or inevitable in your current situation? Write it down specifically.

2. **Question Whose Interests It Serves (1 minute):** Who benefits from this limitation staying in place? What would change if this constraint disappeared?

3. **Imagine the Ideal (1 minute):** If this constraint vanished tomorrow, what would become possible? Don't worry about how—just envision what.

4. **Find the Experiment:** Identify one small action that moves toward the ideal, even if it doesn't solve everything.

118

This isn't naive optimism, but what we might call "strategic rebellion"—the disciplined refusal to accept harmful limitations as permanent features of reality.

When Maya, the program director from Chapter 6, first used this practice with her funding crisis, she realized that the "impossible" constraint wasn't actually the money shortage but the assumption that programs had to be delivered through traditional organizational structures. This insight led to a partnership model that maintained program quality while reducing costs, a solution that emerged only when she questioned the necessity of constraints everyone had accepted as fixed.

The practice works because it distinguishes between genuine limitations (physics, biology, finite resources) and constructed boundaries (policies, traditions, power arrangements). Often what feels impossible is actually just well-protected. This kind of strategic rebellion—the disciplined refusal to accept harmful limitations as permanent features of reality—becomes a core expression of Einfühlung in action.

7.6 From Dreaming to Doing

Imagination—the daring to dream—transforms Einfühlung from mere awareness to generative possibility. Without it, sensing remains trapped in current conditions, discernment becomes mere analysis, and response defaults to habitual patterns. With it, we envision alternatives to present limitations, generate creative tensions that drive meaningful change, collaborate across differences to discover emergent possibilities, and create futures compelling enough to inspire genuine commitment.

The path of imagination isn't simple. It demands what Martha Nussbaum calls "the intelligence of emotions"—the integration of rational analysis with authentic care, of clear-eyed assessment with compelling vision (Nussbaum, 2001). This integration doesn't guarantee immediate transformation but creates the essential tension between what is and what might be, the creative dissonance from which meaningful change emerges.

Yet imagination carries risks. Visionary thinking divorced from constraint can become utopianism—inspiring but ultimately disconnected from the realities that discernment helps us navigate. This is why imagination works best in concert with the other capacities: sensing keeps it grounded in current truth, discernment ensures it remains feasible, and response translates it into concrete action.

Imagination alone doesn't change the world. But it's how we come to believe that change is possible. It names the tension between what is and what could be. It stretches the boundaries of the doable. Yet for dreams to matter, they must move. That's why our next step, response, is where the vision becomes real.

But imagination without action becomes mere fantasy, inspiring perhaps, but ultimately irrelevant to the suffering it hoped to address. The bridge from envisioning to implementing requires our next capacity: response. Having developed the courage to envision beyond current limitations, we're ready to translate possibility into action. To dream is easy. To act on that dream is the real test.

As we turn to exploring response in the next chapter, we carry forward this understanding: imagination isn't opposed to practical action but its essential foundation. The daring to dream gives discipline its direction, action its meaning, and leadership its most enduring impact.

Imagination doesn't escape reality: it stretches it. But only when guided by discernment, fueled by care, and followed by action. Like Proust's "new eyes," empathic imagination doesn't discover different landscapes but reveals possibilities that were always there, waiting for the moral courage to see them.

Chapter 8

RESPOND

The Integrity to Act

What you do speaks so loudly, I cannot hear
what you say.
—Ralph Waldo Emerson

There comes a moment when what we know demands something of us. That moment is response.

Defining Response in the Context of Einfühlung

Before exploring how response manifests in empathic practice, we must clarify what we mean by response within the framework of Einfühlung. Throughout this book, when we refer to "empathy," we mean Einfühlung—a comprehensive approach that integrates sensing, discernment, imagination, and response rather than simple emotional mirroring or sympathy.

Response represents the fourth capacity of Einfühlung: the integrity to act on what we've sensed, discerned, and imagined. Unlike reactions driven by urgency or emotion, empathic response arises from integrating all prior capacities. It's action grounded in deep sensing, informed by wise discernment, and directed by moral imagination.

Response as Embodied Integration: Within Einfühlung, response transforms awareness into action, possibility into reality, understanding into impact. Response is the embodiment, the manifestation of empathy in motion that prevents empathy from remaining mere sentiment and ensures it manifests as concrete choices, behaviors, and commitments that serve human flourishing.

Response as Courageous Witness: Response within Einfühlung requires costly truth-telling—the willingness to act on uncomfortable truths that challenge established power or comfort. This differs from mere activism by maintaining the empathic grounding of sensing and the wisdom of discernment.

Response as Systemic Engagement: Einfühlung's response recognizes that individual actions occur within complex systems. It seeks not just personal integrity but systemic change, acting in ways that honor both immediate needs and long-term transformation.

In this framework, response becomes the bridge between empathic understanding and tangible change, the capacity that transforms "I understand your suffering" into "I will act to address it."

8.1 The Bridge From Seeing to Doing

Elaine Chen admitted, "Honestly, I was terrified," reflecting on her decision to challenge her company's plan to outsource manufacturing despite projected cost savings. "The financial case seemed compelling, and questioning it risked my reputation and relationships. But I couldn't ignore what we'd learned visiting those communities where our plants operated, how our presence created economic stability far beyond direct employment. The spread-sheets didn't capture that reality."

Despite significant pressure, Chen advocated for an alternative approach that maintained domestic manufacturing while implementing targeted efficiency improvements. Her stance wasn't mere opposition but a more complete perspective that incorporated both financial considerations and community impact. Chen explained, "I wasn't arguing against profitability. I was arguing for seeing the complete picture, for recognizing human realities the financial models missed."

The resulting compromise, maintaining domestic production with significant operational changes, proved successful both financially and socially. But for Chen, the most important outcome wasn't the specific decision, but the expanded conversation it generated about how the company evaluated success. She reflected, "We didn't just make a better tactical choice. We started reimagining what 'better' actually means."

Chen's story illustrates a fundamental truth: empathy is incomplete without response. Awareness that doesn't translate into action falls short of its transformative potential. This transition from empathic awareness to courageous action represents one of leadership's most crucial and challenging movements: the bridge between what we've come to understand and what we're willing to do about it.

After sensing, discerning, and imagining comes the moment of truth: when awareness, judgment, and vision must translate into tangible action. We call this capacity response—the integrity to act on what we've sensed, discerned, and imagined, to bring possibility into reality through concrete choices, behaviors, and commitments. Without response, empathy remains mere sentiment, discernment becomes abstract judgment, and imagination degenerates into fantasy. Response gives empathy form—turning awareness into impact.

Response, Not Reaction

The bridge metaphor captures the essence of response: the structure that connects understanding to action, possibility to reality, intention to impact. Like a physical bridge, response must be both solid and flexible, both structurally sound and responsive to changing conditions. It must withstand pressure while adapting to the terrain it crosses.

What makes this bridge so challenging to construct is precisely what makes it so valuable: it connects territories that often seem impossibly distant in organizational life—the territory of human understanding and the territory of tangible action. Building this connection requires not just technical skill but moral courage: the willingness to act on what we've sensed, discerned, and imagined even when doing so involves risk, resistance, or uncertainty.

In GOALS, I wrote that the value of a goal lies less in its achievement than in its orientation—it gives motion to meaning (Morgan, 2025). Responding empathically isn't about heroic leaps; it's about making consistent moves in the direction of what matters. Action need not be perfect to be powerful.

The Courage to Witness Uncomfortable Truths

Empathic response begins with costly truth-telling—the willingness to name realities that challenge organizational narratives, established power arrangements, or comfortable assumptions (Bonhoeffer, 1959). This kind of witness goes beyond criticism by combining clarity with constructive possibility, identifying problems while illuminating paths forward.

What makes such witness "costly" is precisely its challenge to established power and comfort. Research on moral courage shows that truth-telling in organizations typically involves vertical communication across power differentials, creating inherent risk for those with less formal authority (Goodstein,

2015). Hierarchical organizations systematically filter uncomfortable truths, with potentially disruptive information rarely reaching decision-makers unless someone assumes personal risk to ensure its transmission.

This phenomenon explains why historian and Holocaust scholar Deborah Lipstadt emphasizes that "silence is never neutral" when power imbalances exist (Lipstadt, 2019). In such contexts, failing to respond to what we've sensed doesn't merely maintain the status quo but actively reinforces it, communicating tacit approval through our silence. As Lipstadt notes, "Not speaking becomes a form of speaking; not acting becomes a form of acting."

From Empathic Distress to Empathic Concern

Not all emotional responses to others' suffering lead to constructive action. Psychologist Paul Bloom distinguishes between "empathic distress"—becoming emotionally overwhelmed by others' suffering without constructive response—and "empathic concern"—emotional engagement that motivates effective action (Bloom, 2016). Bloom's research demonstrates that empathic distress often leads to avoidance, emotional exhaustion, or ineffective helping behaviors motivated more by relieving personal discomfort than addressing underlying causes.

Transforming distress into concern requires compassionate detachment—the capacity to remain emotionally connected while maintaining sufficient psychological distance for effective response (Goleman, 1998). This balance fosters true altruism: help motivated by care, not discomfort (Batson, 2011).

The bridge from empathy to action isn't built through emotional intensity alone but through the integration of feeling and discernment, connection and boundary, compassion and capacity. This integration doesn't diminish empathy's power but channels it, creating sustainable pathways for impact rather than exhausting flares of concern that ultimately burn out.

Pause to reflect: Think about a time when you felt moved by others' struggles but didn't take action. What barriers stood between your awareness and your response? What might have helped you build the bridge between understanding and action?

8.2 From Knowing-Doing Gap to Courageous Practice

The Keystone: Alignment Amid Complexity

Marcus Thompson reflected, "I began with such clarity," who left a corporate role to lead a nonprofit addressing homelessness. "I had strong values, a clear vision, and what seemed like a straightforward path. Then I encountered reality's resistance—limited resources, competing stakeholder expectations, policy constraints, community politics. Suddenly, my clear values faced a murky implementation landscape where every option involved uncomfortable tradeoffs."

Thompson's experience wasn't unusual. It reflected what happens when abstract values encounter concrete constraints, when clear principles meet complex realities, when theoretical commitments face practical limitations. In this transitional space between values and implementation, integrity faces its greatest test. As Thompson noted, "The real challenge wasn't maintaining my values in theory but expressing them amid constraints that made perfect implementation impossible. I needed integrity not as moral purity, but as coherence in complexity."

Thompson's reflection highlights a crucial aspect of empathic response: the challenging transition from clear values to messy implementation. This phase represents the territory where abstract commitments encounter concrete constraints, where theoretical clarity meets practical complexity. Navigating this territory requires a more nuanced understanding of integrity than simple consistency between stated values and visible behaviors.

The challenge of maintaining integrity amid complexity isn't merely theoretical. I encountered this directly while leading a culture change initiative at a manufacturing organization, as I describe in Designing in the Dark. The culture had become toxic—employees walking on eggshells, innovation stifled by fear, talented people leaving rather than endure the environment. But those who had helped create these conditions held significant influence and persistently pushed back against change efforts, escalating complaints to human resources and directly to the CEO.

As resistance intensified, I watched the CEO waver. The old guard was vocal, organized, and politically savvy. They framed culture change as unnecessary disruption, questioned the costs, and positioned themselves as defenders of "what works." Meanwhile, the employees suffering under the toxic dynamics remained largely silent—not because they didn't want change, but because they'd learned that speaking up brought consequences.

The turning point came during a private conversation with the CEO. After listening to him express concerns about the pushback, I made a choice that felt both necessary and risky. "With respect," I said, "what I'm hearing is that you lack the moral courage to stay the course and challenge these false assumptions. The people defending this culture are the ones who created it. Of course they're going to resist. But your silence in the face of their pressure is being interpreted as validation of their position."

The room went quiet. I had crossed a line—challenging not just his decision but his character, his fundamental capacity for leadership. It was costly truth-telling in its most direct form, the kind of response that either catalyzes breakthrough or ends relationships.

What followed wasn't immediate transformation. The CEO needed time to process the challenge. Some relationships were strained. The political dynamics became more complex. But something had shifted—the uncomfortable truth had been named, and it couldn't be unnamed. Over the following months, the CEO found his courage, the culture change gained momentum, and the organization slowly became a place where people could do their best work.

Reflecting on that moment, I realize I was practicing empathic response in its most challenging form—acting not just on behalf of those being harmed, but in service of a leader who needed to confront his own limitations. The response emerged from sensing the pain of employees caught in a toxic system, discerning that sustainable change required courage at the top, and imagining a workplace where people could flourish rather than merely survive.

Integrity lived not in the confrontation—but in the willingness to risk comfort for truth, to speak for those who couldn't speak for themselves, and to trust that authentic challenge could serve everyone—even those being challenged.

From Moral Purity to Coherent Integrity

Conventional approaches to integrity emphasize consistency—alignment between words and actions, proclaimed values and visible behaviors, stated commitments and actual choices. While valuable as a starting point, this understanding falls short when confronting complex realities where perfect consistency proves impossible due to competing values, resource constraints, or systemic limitations.

A more robust approach frames integrity not as rigid consistency but as coherence under constraint—maintaining alignment between core commitments and concrete actions despite limitations that make perfect implementation impossible (Walker, 2007). This view acknowledges that integrity rarely appears as flawless expression but as the best possible embodiment given real-world constraints.

Research on moral integrity by Angela Duckworth supports this understanding through her concept of "grit with flexibility"—the capacity to maintain principled direction while adapting specific actions to changing circumstances (Duckworth, 2016). Duckworth's research demonstrates that sustainable integrity involves not rigidity but responsiveness, maintaining core commitments while adjusting specific expressions to fit particular contexts and constraints.

The keystone that holds the bridge of response together isn't perfect alignment but coherent adaptation: the capacity to maintain fidelity to core values while navigating the messy realities of actual implementation. Like a keystone in a physical bridge, this coherence doesn't eliminate tension but transforms it, using the opposing forces to create stability rather than allowing them to collapse the structure.

Discernment in Action: Right vs. Right Dilemmas

Joseph Badaracco identifies "right-versus-right" scenarios— situations where multiple legitimate values compete, where every option honors some commitments while compromising others (Badaracco, 1997). His research demonstrates that the most challenging leadership choices rarely involve clear right-versus-wrong decisions but rather conflicts between competing goods:

129

- Loyalty to individuals vs. fairness to groups
- Short-term compassion vs. long-term sustainability
- Transparency vs. confidentiality
- Innovation vs. stability
- Individual autonomy vs. collective welfare

These dilemmas require moral imagination—the capacity to find creative paths that honor multiple values even if imperfectly, rather than defaulting to simplistic either/or choices.

From Either/Or to Both/And Thinking

Navigating the risk of alignment often requires shifting from "either/or" to "both/and" thinking, moving beyond false dichotomies toward integrative thinking (Martin, 2009). Roger Martin's research on effective leadership demonstrates that those who maintain integrity amid complexity rarely choose between competing values but create new options that honor multiple priorities simultaneously, even if imperfectly.

This capacity appears in what Robert Kegan describes as "fifth-order consciousness"—the ability to hold contradictions not as problems to resolve but as polarities to navigate (Kegan, 1994). Kegan's research shows that this consciousness enables leaders to transcend false choices between competing goods, identifying creative paths that honor multiple values rather than sacrificing some for others.

The both/and approach doesn't eliminate difficult choices but transforms how we approach them, seeking not perfect solutions but right-versus-right discernment. This approach recognizes that the most challenging leadership choices involve not clear right-versus-wrong scenarios but conflicts between legitimate goods, situations where every option honors some values while compromising others.

This is what integrity looks like in the real world: not choosing one value, but learning to carry the weight of two.

8.3 Acting in Complexity: From Reaction to Response

The Spider's Web: Response in Complex Systems

Dr. Ananya Gupta admitted, "We kept implementing 'solutions' that became the source of new problems," who led a healthcare improvement initiative in a large hospital system. "Solving ER staffing created new bottlenecks in inpatient units. We'd improve diagnostic protocols, only to generate treatment delays. Each intervention worked locally but triggered unanticipated consequences elsewhere in the system."

The breakthrough came when Dr. Gupta's team shifted from isolated fixes to whole-system seeing—understanding the hospital as an interconnected network rather than a collection of separate departments and functions. We stopped asking "How do we fix this?" and started asking "How is this connected?" This approach led to interventions designed not as definitive solutions but as "probes"—actions implemented to learn how the system would respond, generating insights that informed subsequent adaptations.

Dr. Gupta reflected, "The most important change was conceptual. We abandoned the illusion of solving complex problems once and for all, and instead embraced continuous responsiveness, making smaller, more frequent adjustments based on real-time feedback about how the system was actually behaving, not how we thought it should behave."

Dr. Gupta's experience illustrates a crucial truth about empathic response: complex challenges require fundamentally different approaches than complicated ones. While complicated problems (however difficult) can be "solved" through sufficient expertise and resources, complex problems involve too many interacting variables and feedback loops for linear solutions to prove effective. Responding to such complexity demands not more sophisticated solutions but different modes of engagement altogether.

Systemic Response Requires Systemic Awareness

Leadership scholars Ronald Heifetz and Marty Linsky distinguish between "technical problems"—challenges solvable through existing expertise and authority structures—and "adaptive challenges"—issues requiring new learning, perspective shifts, and changes in values or behaviors (Heifetz & Linsky, 2002). Their research demonstrates that the most significant leadership failures occur not from lack of effort but from applying technical approaches to adaptive challenges, attempting to solve through expertise what actually requires learning and adaptation.

This distinction aligns with the Cynefin framework developed by Dave Snowden and Mary Boone, which differentiates between "complicated" domains (where cause-effect relationships exist but may require expertise to discern) and "complex" domains (where cause-effect relationships cannot be determined in advance but only understood in retrospect) (Snowden & Boone, 2007). Research shows that approaches effective in complicated contexts—like best practices, expert analysis, and comprehensive planning—actually increase failure risk when applied to complex challenges.

The implications for empathic response are profound. Rather than seeking more sophisticated analyses or comprehensive solutions, effective response in complex systems requires dancing with systems—engaging through iterative learning rather than definitive fixing, through emergent adaptation rather than predetermined implementation, through continuous responsiveness rather than discrete intervention (Meadows, 1999).

From Planning to Probing

When cause-effect relationships cannot be determined in advance, conventional planning approaches—which assume predictable relationships between actions and outcomes—become not merely ineffective but actively misleading. They create the illusion of control, the false confidence that complexity can be managed through planning alone (Ackoff, 1994).

A more effective approach employs probe-sense-respond cycles—small interventions designed not as solutions but as experiments to reveal how the system actually functions (Uhl-Bien & Marion, 2009). These probes serve as safe-to-fail experiments: limited actions with sufficient scale to generate meaningful learning but insufficient scale to create catastrophic consequences if unsuccessful (Westley et al., 2006).

This experimental approach embodies execution-as-learning—viewing implementation not as the application of predetermined solutions but as the testing of hypotheses about what might work (Edmondson, 2019). Amy Edmondson's research on organizational learning demonstrates that this approach significantly outperforms traditional execution-as-efficiency models when addressing novel or complex challenges precisely because it treats unexpected outcomes not as implementation failures but as valuable learning that informs subsequent responses.

As I explored in GOALS, what sustains long-term change isn't constant motivation—it's the discipline of returning, again and again, to what matters most (Morgan, 2025). Small wins build confidence. Setbacks test your why. Courage becomes less about dramatic gestures and more about choosing the next right step, even when it's the harder one.

8.4 The Echoing Voice: Stories That Amplify Impact

Eduardo Vasquez reflected, "The case study transformed the conversation," an organizational development consultant. "For months, we'd been discussing the need for more empathetic leadership in abstract terms, with little traction. Then we shared Sonia's story—how she restructured decision-making processes to include frontline voices, the resistance she encountered, the moments she almost abandoned the effort, and the breakthrough that eventually came. Suddenly, theoretical concepts became tangible possibilities."

The impact went beyond intellectual understanding. As Vasquez noted, "People didn't just comprehend empathic leadership better—they could envision themselves implementing it. The story made courage contagious because it made it concrete. It transformed empathy from an abstract virtue into a practical path with specific markers, challenges, and possibilities."

Vasquez's observation highlights a crucial dimension of empathic response: its narrative power. Beyond implementing specific actions, response involves creating stories that make courage visible, narratives that translate abstract empathy into concrete examples that inspire broader transformation. These stories don't just illustrate—they invite, making empathic action seem not just admirable but possible, not just exceptional but achievable.

Stories That Move Systems

The power of stories in translating empathy to action reflects what narrative psychologist Jerome Bruner identifies as the fundamental narrative structure of human meaning-making (Bruner, 1990). Bruner's research demonstrates that humans understand experience primarily through narrative rather than analytical frameworks, integrating events into stories that establish causality, purpose, and significance rather than merely processing isolated information.

This narrative orientation explains why organizational learning expert Stephen Denning found that analytical presentations rarely catalyze significant change, while well-crafted stories often do (Denning, 2011). Denning's research shows that while analysis can impart information, stories create narrative transportation—the psychological state where listeners imaginatively enter the narrative world, experiencing emotions and insights that analytical presentation rarely generates.

For empathic response, this distinction proves crucial. While analytical explanations of empathic principles may generate intellectual agreement, stories of empathic action create empathic resonance—the state where others don't merely understand empathy conceptually but experience it directly through narrative engagement, creating both emotional connection and practical inspiration (Brown, 2018).

From Exceptional Heroes to Accessible Models

Traditional organizational narratives often highlight exceptional individuals performing extraordinary acts—the CEO who risked everything on a bold vision, the whistleblower who sacrificed career for principle, the innovator who persisted despite universal skepticism. While inspiring, such narratives can actually diminish response by creating low self-efficacy: the belief that such actions lie beyond one's own capacity (Bandura, 1997).

More effective narratives feature accessible heroes—individuals similar enough to the audience that their actions seem attainable rather than exceptional (Drayton, 2010). Research on social innovation demonstrates that changemaking spreads not through admiration of extraordinary figures, but through identification with relatable models whose courage seems replicable in one's own context.

This principle explains why organizational change expert John Kotter emphasizes "small-scale success stories" in transformation efforts (Kotter, 2008). Kotter's research shows that these narratives prove more effective than grand vision statements precisely because they make change tangible and accessible, demonstrating specific, implementable actions rather than abstract aspirations.

The Power of Vulnerability in Leadership Narratives

Counterintuitively, the most influential stories of empathic response often highlight not flawless implementation but authentic struggle, including moments of doubt, resistance, and imperfect execution. Research demonstrates that these "vulnerable narratives" generate greater response than stories of untroubled success precisely because they create psychological accessibility— making courage seem attainable despite inevitable challenges rather than requiring perfect capacity (Grant, 2017).

Brené Brown extends this understanding through her research on rumbling with vulnerability (Brown, 2018). Brown's work shows that leaders who acknowledge their struggles while maintaining commitment generate more creative cultures than those who project invulnerability, precisely because shared struggle validates others' experience and shows that difficulty doesn't preclude progress.

This vulnerable approach requires truth-telling without truth-claiming—honest sharing of one's experience without presenting it as universal or definitive (Frank, 2010). Research on effective narrative demonstrates that stories inspire action most powerfully when they offer witness rather than blueprint: authentic testimony that invites others' engagement rather than prescriptive instruction that positions the narrator as authoritative expert.

8.5 Practices for Sustained Response

The Response Readiness Practice

When facing a situation that calls for empathic action, use this practice to ensure your response emerges from Einfühlung rather than reaction:

1. **Ground in Sensing (2 minutes):** What are you sensing about this situation beyond the obvious? What signals are you picking up about unspoken needs, systemic patterns, or emerging possibilities?

2. **Apply Discernment (2 minutes):** Among the possible responses, which ones honor multiple stakeholders? What would wise action look like that maintains integrity while adapting to constraints?

3. **Connect to Imagination (1 minute):** How does this response serve the larger vision of what's possible? What story might this action tell about the kind of change you're working toward?

4. **Choose Your Response:** Select the action that best integrates your sensing, discernment, and imagination, even if it's imperfect or incomplete.

This practice grounds response in Einfühlung rather than just urgency, emotion, or habit. It prepares you not just for effective action but for sustainable action, a response that can be maintained over time through the fifth capacity of replenishment.

Reflection question: Think about a story of courageous action that has influenced you. What made it powerful? How did it balance inspiration with accessibility? How might you share your own stories of response in ways that invite rather than intimidate others?

Action isn't the opposite of empathy. It's what gives it integrity.

"Don't wait for the moment to feel right. Let the act itself make it right. Every step aligned with purpose becomes a vote for the future you believe in." —David Morgan, 2025

8.6 From Response to Replenishment

Response—the integrity to act—transforms empathy from mere sentiment into tangible impact. Without it, sensing remains passive awareness, discernment becomes abstract judgment, and imagination degenerates into fantasy. With it, empathy manifests as concrete choices, behaviors, and commitments that change both external conditions and internal realities.

The path of response isn't simple. It demands what Martha Nussbaum calls "perceptive equilibrium"—the integration of clear principles with contextual wisdom, of steadfast commitment with adaptive responsiveness, of confident action with genuine humility (Nussbaum, 2001). This integration doesn't guarantee perfect outcomes but creates the conditions for meaningful change, the foundation that makes transformation not just possible—but real.

This transformation prepares us for the fifth and final capacity in our Human Engine: replenishment. Having developed the integrity to act on what we've sensed, discerned, and imagined, we must now cultivate the wisdom to sustain, to maintain empathic response not as occasional heroism but as ongoing practice. Without replenishment, response becomes depleting, creating patterns of exhaustion, cynicism, and withdrawal that ultimately undermine the very commitments that inspired action. With it, response becomes sustainable, anchored in practices that renew capacity even as it's expended.

As we turn to exploring replenishment in the next chapter, we carry forward this understanding: that integrity doesn't require perfect implementation but committed presence, showing up fully even amid limitations, maintaining coherence even amid complexity, and embodying values even when their perfect expression proves impossible. The integrity to act doesn't eliminate struggle but gives it meaning, purpose, and ultimately, impact.

Replenishment is not rest alone. It is design for renewal. It is how we honor what matters most, again, and again, and again.

Chapter 9

REPLENISH

The Rhythm That Renews

"We cannot serve from an empty vessel."
—Eleanor Brown

In a world that rewards urgency and punishes rest, leaders often mistake endurance for effectiveness. But sustainable leadership is not about lasting longer; it's about leading in ways that can be sustained.

After learning to sense what systems can't yet say, discern wisely amid complexity, imagine beyond current constraints, and respond with integrity, we arrive at the capacity that sustains all others: replenishment. Without this wisdom to sustain, even the most profound empathic abilities eventually deteriorate. With it, empathy becomes not heroic effort but ongoing way of being.

This chapter explores how to create rhythms that integrate engagement and renewal, why communities matter more than individual resilience, and how purpose itself can become a source of restoration. We'll discover that empathy is sustained not through endurance, but through rhythm: the courage to receive as generously as we give.

Sustainability is not a state; it's a practice of becoming.

9.1 The Breaking Point

The email arrived at 11:47 PM on a Tuesday. Another crisis, another urgent decision needed by morning. Sophia Martinez stared at her phone, feeling the familiar knot in her stomach—not from the problem itself, but from her own reaction to it. Six months ago, this same challenge would have energized her. Tonight, it felt like one more weight on an already strained foundation.

"I realized I was treating sustainability like a math problem," Sophia later reflected on her journey through executive burnout. As director of a nonprofit providing legal aid to underserved communities, her passion for the mission had never wavered. But something fundamental had shifted. "I kept trying to find the perfect allocation of hours, as if the right ratio of work time to personal time would solve everything. But that approach actually made things worse because it treated work and life as opponents in a zero-sum competition for my time."

The breaking point came after a particularly grueling quarter. Despite her commitment to the organization's mission, Sophia found herself dreading meetings, snapping at colleagues, and lying awake at night, simultaneously exhausted and unable to rest. What terrified her most wasn't the fatigue itself but the growing numbness: the sense that her empathy, once so natural, was being replaced by a protective detachment she didn't recognize.

"I was becoming what I had once resisted: someone treating people like cases instead of human beings."

The breakthrough came when Sophia shifted from "balance" to "rhythm," recognizing that sustainable engagement requires not static division but dynamic alternation between different kinds of activity.

"I stopped seeing work and renewal as competitors and started seeing them as partners in a dance. The question wasn't 'How do I balance them?' but 'How do I sequence them in ways that allow each to strengthen the other?'"

This reframing transformed Sophia's approach to sustainability. Rather than attempting to carve out separate domains for work and recovery, she began incorporating rhythms of engagement and renewal throughout her day, week, and year. Brief moments of mindfulness between meetings. A midweek morning dedicated to reflection and strategic thinking. Quarterly retreats for deeper restoration. Annual sabbatical periods for renewal and perspective.

Sophia recognized that rhythms can't thrive in isolation; they require communal understanding and support.

"The most significant change was conceptual," Sophia reflected. "I stopped seeing replenishment as what happens when work stops and started seeing it as an essential component of work itself: not the opposite of productivity but its necessary foundation."

Sophia's shift was more than a lifestyle tweak; it was the final turning of a larger wheel. After the sensing, discerning, imagining, and acting of earlier chapters, this was the part too many leaders overlook: the part where we begin again. Replenishment completes the empathic cycle by preparing us to start it anew: clearer, stronger, and more whole.

What Is Replenishment?

Replenishment is the wisdom to sustain empathic engagement over time—not through heroic endurance but through intentional rhythms that integrate engagement and renewal, individual practice and communal support, personal restoration and purpose connection.

Sophia's shift illustrates a fundamental truth: sustainable empathy requires not balance but rhythm, not the static division of time between engagement and renewal but their dynamic integration through intentional patterns of activity and rest. After sensing, discerning, imagining, and responding comes the final, often neglected capacity that completes the empathic cycle: replenishment, the wisdom to sustain empathic engagement not as occasional heroism but as ongoing practice.

We cannot pour from empty vessels. But we can design systems that keep vessels full.

9.2 Learning to Listen: The Language of Depletion

Recognizing the Signals

Dr. Sarah Kim had always prided herself on reading people well—sensing when patients were anxious, when colleagues were overwhelmed, when her team needed support. But she'd never learned to read herself. "I kept pushing through the signals," she reflected on her journey through physician burnout. "The tension headaches, the irritability at home, the way I'd started dreading patient interactions. I treated these as obstacles to overcome rather than information to heed."

The turning point came during a particularly difficult week when a colleague gently asked, "Sarah, when's the last time you took a real breath?" The question stopped her cold. She realized she'd been holding her breath—literally and figuratively—for months.

"I had to learn that my body and mind were trying to tell me something important. The exhaustion wasn't weakness; it was information. The cynicism creeping in wasn't character failure but a warning system trying to protect something precious: my capacity to care."

Our bodies speak in whispers before they shout. Learning to listen to these early signals—the slight tension in our shoulders, the moments when empathy feels forced rather than natural, the urge to avoid rather than engage—becomes essential intelligence for sustainable leadership.

Research by trauma specialist Bessel van der Kolk reveals that chronic empathic stress creates patterns similar to trauma, storing emotional residue in our nervous system and body (van der Kolk, 2014). When we consistently absorb others' emotions without proper processing, our system begins to protect itself through gradual shutdown.

The signals often follow a predictable progression:

- **Early whispers:** Slight fatigue, needing more caffeine, feeling "off"

- **Clearer conversations:** Irritability, decision fatigue, avoiding certain people or tasks

- **Urgent shouts:** Emotional numbness, physical symptoms, cynicism about work that once inspired us

Three Depths of Recovery

Rather than treating all depletion the same way, sustainable leaders learn to match their recovery response to the depth of their need. Drawing from breakthrough research on performance and stress recovery, three distinct levels of restoration emerge—each serving a different function in maintaining empathic capacity.

9.3 Micro-Recovery: The Art of the Reset

When Dr. Kim first learned about micro-recovery, she was skeptical. "Ninety seconds? That's not going to fix months of exhaustion." But her coach encouraged her to experiment: "What if you treated these moments not as solutions but as preventions? What if the goal isn't to recover from burnout, but to prevent its accumulation?"

Performance researcher Steven Kotler describes this as the recovery phase of the flow cycle: brief periods that allow our neurochemical systems to reset before depletion compounds (Kotler, 2021). During intense empathic engagement, our brains produce a cascade of stress hormones and neurochemicals. Without micro-recovery, these accumulate, gradually narrowing our bandwidth for complex thinking and emotional regulation.

Dr. Kim started with non-time: 60 to 90 seconds of simply being present without agenda. Between patient visits, instead of immediately reviewing charts, she would take three conscious breaths and briefly connect with her intention to heal. "It wasn't meditation," she clarified. "It was more like... remembering who I was underneath the urgency."

The results surprised her. "Those tiny moments created space I didn't know I needed. Not just to rest, but to transition. To let go of the previous interaction and show up fresh for the next one."

Kotler's research reveals why these brief interventions prove so powerful: they interrupt the cascade of stress hormones while they're still manageable, preventing the compound accumulation that leads to burnout. The key is consistency rather than duration—90 seconds of genuine presence repeated throughout the day proves more restorative than longer periods of forced relaxation.

Micro-Recovery Practices:
- Three conscious breaths between meetings or interactions

- Brief grounding moments: feeling feet on floor, noticing one thing you can see, hear, smell
- Intention reset: asking "How do I want to show up for this next interaction?"
- Gratitude pause: naming one thing you appreciate about your work or the person you just helped

9.4 Active Recovery: Completing the Stress Cycle

Marcus Rivera, a social worker in child protective services, discovered that his evening runs weren't just exercise—they were emotional processing. "I'd carry the weight of what I'd seen that day in my body. The running somehow helped me... release it. Not forget it, but metabolize it."

Marcus had unknowingly discovered completing the stress cycle (Nagoski & Nagoski, 2019). Their groundbreaking work on burnout reveals that empathic professionals often absorb emotional stress without ever processing it to completion. The stress gets stuck in our system, accumulating like sediment in a river.

The Nagoski sisters' research demonstrates that stress has a biological cycle requiring physical completion. When we witness others' pain, our nervous system activates as if the threat were our own. But unlike our ancestors who could run from or fight actual dangers, empathic professionals must sit with emotional pain without physical release. This creates unfinished stress cycles: emotional activation without resolution.

"Physical activity isn't just good for our health," Emily Nagoski explains. "It's how we close the loop on emotional stress." The research shows that 20 minutes of movement—walking, dancing, even vigorous cleaning—can metabolize stress hormones and return our nervous system to baseline.

Marcus found that his runs became a ritual of transition. "The first mile was usually heavy—I could feel the day in my legs, my shoulders. But somewhere around mile two, something would shift. By the end, I felt... clear. Not because the problems were solved, but because I'd processed my response to them."

Beyond physical movement, the Nagoski sisters identify other powerful cycle-completion strategies:

Creative Expression: Art, music, writing help process emotions that words alone cannot capture. A nurse manager started spending 15 minutes each evening sketching—not to create art, but to externalize the emotional complexity of her day.

Positive Social Connection: Brief but genuine human connection—a hug from a family member, a real conversation with a friend—signals to our nervous system that we're safe and supported. Research shows that 20 seconds of physical affection can significantly lower cortisol levels.

Emotional Release: Crying, laughing, or even controlled anger (like punching a pillow) helps discharge accumulated emotional energy. Many cultures have rituals for this—keening, celebration, communal expression of grief or joy.

The key insight from the Nagoski sisters: we don't heal from empathic exhaustion by avoiding emotions but by completing our emotional responses to them.

The Moral Consequences of Depletion

"I kept treating self-care as a luxury, something I'd get to if time permitted after addressing everyone else's needs," admitted Gabriel Wong, a healthcare administrator who found himself increasingly exhausted despite his commitment to compassionate leadership. "What changed my perspective was a conversation with a mentor who asked a simple but profound question: 'What's the impact on others when your empathy is depleted? Who suffers when you have nothing left to give?'"

This reframing transformed Wong's approach to replenishment. Rather than seeing it as personal indulgence that took time away from service to others, he recognized it as a moral responsibility that enabled sustainable service.

"I realized that chronic depletion wasn't noble but harmful—both to myself and to those I was trying to serve. Renewal wasn't selfish but essential to continued care for others."

Depletion is not only a personal hazard; it's an ethical one. When leaders operate from a state of exhaustion, their moral reasoning deteriorates, empathy distorts, and unintended harm increases.

The ethical implications extend beyond individual wellbeing to organizational innovation capacity. When leaders operate from depletion, they gravitate toward familiar solutions rather than exploring creative possibilities. As I note in Generation Innovate, "We don't burn out from caring. We burn out from never stopping. Innovation isn't powered by hustle alone—it's sustained by rhythm" (Morgan, 2025). The courage to strategically constrain certain business elements to create recovery space becomes an investment in the organization's creative potential.

Beyond enabling continued service, replenishment serves as moral discipline by preventing the ethical deterioration that accompanies depletion. Daniel Kahneman's research on decision fatigue demonstrates that moral judgment significantly declines as cognitive and emotional resources diminish, with depleted individuals making more self-protective, less altruistic, and less principled choices than when adequately resourced (Kahneman, 2011).

Research by ethics scholar Ann Tenbrunsel discovered that ethical lapses in organizations increase dramatically during periods of high demand and limited recovery. Tenbrunsel's studies show that depletion creates ethical fading: the decreased accessibility of moral considerations when making decisions under depleted conditions (Tenbrunsel & Smith-Crowe, 2012).

These findings redefine how we see the link between renewal and ethics. Rather than competing priorities, they function as integrated aspects of moral life, with renewal serving as essential discipline for maintaining ethical capacity.

When Depletion Distorts Empathy

A leader who has not replenished can mistake urgency for importance, intensity for connection, and control for clarity. Replenishment isn't just self-care; it's system care. When we lead from depletion, our empathy becomes extraction, demanding from others what we cannot give ourselves. Empathy without replenishment becomes performance. It pulls on reserves we no longer have, converting connection into obligation.

To give what we have not received, to pour from vessels unfilled, to sustain what we cannot nourish: this is not virtue but vanity, not service but its simulation.

What if the deepest generosity is not endless giving, but the courage to receive? What if the truest offering is to honor the rhythms that make giving possible?

9.5 Deep Recovery: Restoring the Foundation

When organizational consultant Diana Chang returned from her first sabbatical in fifteen years, colleagues noticed something different. "She seemed... bigger somehow," one team member observed. "Not physically, but like she was occupying more of herself."

Diana had discovered body-based restoration: recovery practices that address the deep physiological impact of chronic empathic stress (van der Kolk, 2014). After years of carrying others' trauma in her consulting work, Diana realized that weekend rest and even vacation weren't sufficient. Her nervous system needed fundamental recalibration.

"I'd been thinking about recovery as returning to baseline," Diana reflected. "But I realized my baseline had shifted. I'd adapted to a constant state of low-level activation—hypervigilance, always scanning for the next crisis. I needed to remember what calm actually felt like."

Van der Kolk's research reveals that chronic empathic stress creates lasting changes in our nervous system, similar to trauma responses. Our bodies become habituated to activation, losing access to the parasympathetic "rest and digest" state essential for true restoration. Conventional recovery approaches—vacation, entertainment, even exercise—may provide temporary relief but don't address these deeper physiological patterns.

Diana's sabbatical included daily yoga, weekly massage, and long periods in nature. "But the real transformation happened through what my teacher called 'somatic experiencing'— learning to notice and slowly discharge patterns of tension I'd been carrying for years."

Van der Kolk's work demonstrates that body-based practices uniquely access the nervous system's capacity for self-regulation. Unlike cognitive approaches that work through the thinking mind, somatic practices engage the body's innate wisdom for healing and restoration.

Deep Recovery Practices:

Breathwork and Yoga: Conscious breathing practices calm the vagus nerve and activate the parasympathetic nervous system. Van der Kolk's research shows that trauma-informed yoga specifically helps restore emotional regulation capacity.

Nature Immersion: Extended time in natural environments provides what attention restoration theory calls "soft fascination"— gentle stimulation that allows directed attention to recover while maintaining gentle engagement (Kaplan, 1995). Diana found that morning walks in the forest became "conversations with something larger than human problems."

Bodywork and Touch: Massage, acupuncture, or other therapeutic touch help release stored stress patterns and restore healthy nervous system function. Van der Kolk notes that appropriate touch can literally rewire our capacity for emotional regulation.

Creative and Expressive Arts: Dance, theater, art-making engage what van der Kolk calls "right-brain processing"—helping integrate emotional experiences in ways that pure verbal processing cannot achieve.

Retreat and Solitude: Regular periods of extended quiet— whether through meditation retreats, solo travel, or simply unstructured time—allow our system to return to its natural rhythms without external demands.

The distinguishing feature of deep recovery isn't duration but depth—practices that address the fundamental patterns holding stress in our system rather than simply providing temporary relief.

Diana captured it best: "I learned the difference between resting from work and resting into myself. One is temporary relief. The other is restoration of capacity."

The Integration: Building Your Recovery Rhythm

These three levels of recovery work synergistically, each serving a different function in maintaining sustainable empathic capacity:

- **Micro-recovery** prevents daily accumulation of stress

- **Active recovery** processes and completes emotional cycles

- **Deep recovery** restores fundamental nervous system capacity

The art lies not in choosing one approach but in creating rhythms that integrate all three: micro-moments throughout each day, active processing several times per week, and deep restoration seasonally or annually.

Sarah Kim, Marcus Rivera, and Diana Chang each discovered that sustainable empathy requires not just the courage to feel but the wisdom to recover. Their stories remind us that replenishment isn't weakness, but strategic resource management—the foundation that makes continued empathic engagement possible.

9.6 Creating Communities of Renewal

"None of us can sustain this work alone," observed Reverend Darius Jackson, reflecting on how his community organizing coalition had maintained commitment to justice work for over two decades despite significant challenges. "We tried individual approaches to sustainability: encouraging people to practice self-care, to establish boundaries, to develop personal resilience. But we kept losing people to burnout until we recognized that sustainability itself needed to be a collective practice, not just an individual responsibility."

This recognition led to fundamental changes in how the coalition operated. They established regular communal restoration gatherings alongside their justice work. They developed shared practices for marking both progress and loss. They created explicit norms around pace, workload, and recovery. Most significantly, they began treating sustainability not as something individual members should address separately, but as a collective capacity the community cultivated together.

"The most important shift was conceptual," Jackson reflected. "We stopped seeing depletion as personal failure and started recognizing it as a systemic reality requiring communal response. We shifted the question—from 'How do I stay well?' to 'How do we stay well together?'"

Beyond Individual Resilience to Communal Capacity

Contemporary approaches to sustainability often emphasize individual resilience: the personal capacity to withstand challenging conditions without succumbing to burnout or disengagement. While valuable, this framing inadvertently places responsibility for sustainability on individuals rather than on the systems and communities that create the conditions within which people operate.

As resilience researcher Michael Ungar observes, "We've been asking the wrong question. Instead of asking 'Why aren't people more resilient?' we should ask 'Why do we require so much resilience?'" (Ungar, 2019).

Research on sustainable activism by community psychologist Mary Watkins demonstrates that the most effective approach involves communities of resilience rather than resilient individuals (Watkins, 2019). Watkins's studies reveal that sustainability emerges primarily from relational contexts that distribute both burden and renewal, that normalize rather than stigmatize vulnerability, and that treat depletion as communal responsibility rather than personal failure.

Cultural Foundations of Sustainable Communities

Creating communities of renewal requires not just structural changes but cultural transformation: shifting the beliefs, values, and norms that govern organizational life. Research on sustainable organizations demonstrates that the most effective approach involves cultivating cultures of resilience: shared meaning systems that normalize renewal, validate vulnerability, distribute responsibility, and maintain purpose connection even amid challenging circumstances.

The most effective cultures establish cycles of renewal: self-reinforcing patterns where restoration enables more effective engagement, which in turn creates resources for deeper restoration (Dutton, 2006).

What if sustainability isn't primarily an individual achievement but a communal creation? How might this shift in perspective change how you approach renewal in your organization or team?

9.7 Purpose as Ultimate Renewal

"The work itself became my deepest source of renewal," reflected environmental activist Maya Chen, who had maintained passionate engagement through decades of challenging advocacy. "Not because it was easy; it often wasn't. But because it connected me to a purpose larger than myself. The difficulties actually deepened my commitment rather than diminishing it because they confirmed the importance of what we were doing."

Chen's experience contradicted conventional wisdom about sustainability, which often assumes that challenging work inherently depletes while easy work renews. Instead, she found that connection to meaningful purpose provided a form of replenishment that recreational activities or relaxation alone couldn't offer.

"Obviously. I needed regular rest and recovery; I wasn't immune to physical and emotional fatigue. But true restoration came from remembering why the work mattered, from reconnecting with the purpose that made the challenges worth enduring."

The Paradox of Meaningful Engagement

Research by psychologist Christina Maslach reveals a seeming paradox: some of the most challenging work produces not greater burnout, but deeper engagement when connected to clear purpose. Maslach's studies demonstrate that the relationship between difficulty and depletion isn't linear; work can be simultaneously demanding and sustaining when individuals experience meaningful depletion: expenditure of energy for purposes they genuinely value (Maslach, 2017).

This paradox appears in flow researcher Mihaly Csikszentmihalyi's discoveries about optimal experience: that humans find greatest fulfillment not in relaxation but in focused engagement with meaningful challenges that match their capacity (Csikszentmihalyi, 1990). His research demonstrates that flow experiences provide a form of rejuvenation that passive recovery cannot replicate.

From Hedonic to Eudaimonic Wellbeing

This purpose dimension reflects the distinction between eudaimonic wellbeing (fulfillment through meaning, purpose, and virtue) versus hedonic wellbeing (pleasure through comfort and enjoyment). While both matter, research by wellbeing expert Carol Ryff demonstrates that eudaimonic approaches correlate more strongly with long-term sustainability, resilience amid challenge, and resistance to burnout (Ryff, 2014).

Applied to empathic leadership, this understanding transforms how we approach replenishment—moving beyond mere comfort toward meaning-centered restoration: renewal that explicitly reconnects individuals with the deeper purposes that make their efforts worthwhile (Wong, 2014).

But purpose alone is not always protective. In the absence of replenishment, even meaningful work can lead to burnout, especially when purpose is used to justify unsustainable conditions. The most dangerous depletion often comes wrapped in noble intentions, when leaders sacrifice their own sustainability on the altar of worthy causes.

9.8 Practices for Rhythmic Leadership

The Rhythm Reset

When to use: When feeling depleted, when urgency overrides everything else, or as daily practice to prevent burnout.

How (3 minutes):

1. **Breathe in what sustains you (1 minute):** Name one thing that genuinely restores your energy: connection, purpose, beauty, movement.

2. **Breathe out what depletes you (1 minute):** Acknowledge what's draining you without trying to fix it; just notice and release.

3. **Choose your rhythm (1 minute):** Rather than forcing constant availability, identify your personal pattern of creative intensity and recovery. As I explore in Generation Innovate, energy operates in waves—some leaders peak in early morning focus, others in late afternoon innovation sessions (Morgan, 2025). Honor these natural rhythms rather than fighting them.

After: Honor that commitment to yourself, not as luxury but as leadership responsibility.

What rhythms naturally restore you: time in nature, meaningful conversation, creative expression, physical movement? How might honoring these rhythms become not just personal care but a form of service to those who depend on your sustained empathy and leadership?

9.9 Completing the Cycle

Just as breath requires both inhalation and exhalation, so too does empathy require both outward engagement and inward renewal. Replenishment completes the cycle of sensing, discerning, imagining, and responding, making it possible to begin again—and begin better.

Replenishment transforms empathy from depleting obligation into sustainable practice. Without it, even the most profound empathic capacities eventually deteriorate: sensing becomes dulled, discernment grows rigid, imagination narrows, and response becomes mechanical. With it, empathy becomes not heroic effort but ongoing way of being—anchored in practices, communities, and purposes that sustain rather than deplete.

The path of replenishment demands the integration of conceptual understanding with embodied practice, of theoretical insight with lived experience (Polanyi, 1962). This integration doesn't eliminate struggle but transforms it: from depleting obstacle to meaningful challenge, from energy drain to purpose confirmation, from sustainability threat to opportunity for deeper commitment.

This transformation completes our Human Engine, bringing us full circle to the beginning. After sensing what systems can't yet say, discerning wisdom amid complexity, imagining possibilities beyond current constraints, and responding with integrity, replenishment doesn't close the empathic cycle; it reopens it. It renews our capacity to sense, discern, imagine, and respond with integrity. Without this completion, the empathic cycle becomes a downward spiral of diminishing capacity. With it, empathy becomes a generative cycle of expanding possibility.

As research on sustainable performance has shown, depth requires intentional rhythms, not constancy. The greater the output, the more essential the renewal.

What restores us, repeats. Over time, rhythm becomes culture.

Empathy is sustained not through endurance but through rhythm. We sense, discern, imagine, respond, and replenish. Again and again. The Human Engine doesn't end; it breathes. And in this breath, we begin again.

As we conclude this exploration of the Human Engine, we carry forward this understanding: that empathy isn't primarily a feeling but a practice, not merely a disposition but a discipline, not just a momentary connection but a sustainable commitment. The wisdom to sustain doesn't replace the courage to engage but enables its continuation, allowing empathy to become not occasional heroism but an ongoing way of being.

To lead with empathy is not to exhaust ourselves in service of others but to circulate the conditions that make empathy possible: noticing, listening, imagining, acting, and restoring. Again and again, this is the work and the way.

The Human Engine is not a static machine but a living cycle. What you nourish today shapes what you'll notice, feel, and create tomorrow.

PART III

SCALING THE SACRED

Where Systems Begin to Breathe

We've explored the internal work of Einfühlung. Now: what happens when we live those practices inside systems not designed to hold them?

Part III is about sacred scaling—not growth or replication, but resonance. When inner coherence meets external complexity. When a leader's presence shifts a room's temperature. When small rituals rewrite norms. When policy becomes porous to what people actually feel.

Scaling empathy isn't about expanding output. It's about creating conditions where connection can propagate.

This section explores how:

- Leadership becomes a sensing instrument
- Culture containers collective regulation
- Resistance becomes intelligence, not friction
- Design becomes sacred repair

No formulas here. But ways of moving through complexity, tuning to signals, tending rhythms, inviting co-evolution.

Empathy in motion. Made cultural. Made collective. Made systemic. Made sustainable.

The sacred doesn't scale by command. It scales by invitation.

Chapter 10

LEADERSHIP PRESENCE

The Foundation for Organizational Einfühlung

"The real voyage of discovery consists not in
seeking new landscapes, but in having new
eyes."
—Marcel Proust

Having explored the five capacities of the Human Engine—
sensing what systems can't yet say, discerning wisdom amid
complexity, imagining beyond current constraints, responding
with integrity, and replenishing sustainably—we arrive at the
question that transforms everything: How do these capacities
become not just personal practices but organizational realities?

This chapter bridges individual development and systemic
transformation. We'll discover how your presence as a leader
creates the conditions where others can access their own
empathic capacities, how the five dimensions work together as
an integrated leadership approach, and how to cultivate
organizational Einfühlung.

The goal isn't to perfect these capacities in isolation, but to embody them in ways that invite others into their own empathic development. Leadership presence becomes the foundation from which individual empathy becomes organizational empathy, personal practice becomes cultural transformation.

10.1 The Moment of Recognition

David Peters felt it the moment he walked into the conference room. Something was different. The quarterly numbers were stellar: revenue up 12%, costs down 3%, market share expanding. Yet the energy in the room felt flat, almost brittle. His leadership team sat around the polished table, posture perfect, smiles professional, but underneath he sensed something else. A current of tension he couldn't quite name.

Six months earlier, David would have pushed through this feeling, focusing on the metrics, celebrating the wins. But this time, he paused. He set down the report and simply said, "Before we dive into the numbers, I'm sensing something in the room. What's happening that I should know about?"

The silence stretched for what felt like minutes. Then Maria, his head of operations, spoke quietly: "David, we've been having conversations about whether this growth is sustainable. People are burning out. We're hitting targets, but we're not sure how much longer we can maintain this pace."

What followed was the most honest conversation David's team had shared in years. They talked about the hidden costs of their success: the weekend work that had become routine, the family dinners missed, creative projects shelved for lack of bandwidth. They discussed the early warning signs they'd been seeing but hadn't felt safe to mention: increased sick days, shortened lunch breaks, how laughter had slowly faded from team meetings.

By the end of that meeting, David and his team had completely reframed their success metrics and developed a sustainability plan that would serve them for years to come. But the transformation didn't begin with strategy or analysis. It began with presence: David's willingness to pause, sense what was actually happening, and create space for truth to emerge.

This is the foundation of empathic leadership: the capacity to be fully present to what is, rather than lost in what should be or focused solely on what was. When leaders cultivate this quality of presence, they create the conditions where Einfühlung becomes possible not just for themselves, but for their entire organization.

10.2 From Presence to Einfühlung: A Leadership Operating System

Most leadership development focuses on what to do: strategies to implement, skills to master, behaviors to adopt. But empathic leadership begins with how to be. Presence is the foundational capacity that enables everything else. Without presence, leadership becomes reactive, superficial, and disconnected from the deeper currents that drive organizational life.

But what kind of empathy emerges from this foundation of presence? Here lies a crucial distinction that transforms how we understand empathic leadership.

Einfühlung, a German term meaning "feeling into," refers to the capacity to sense collective dynamics and emerging patterns within organizational fields, rather than simply understanding individual emotions. It's the ability to feel into the shared experience of a group, team, or entire organization: sensing what wants to emerge, what's being avoided, and what the system as a whole needs to thrive.

Classic Empathy	Einfühlung (Feeling Into)
"I understand how you feel"	"I sense what's happening in this field"
Individual emotional recognition	Systemic pattern sensing
Absorbing others' emotions	Feeling into without taking on
Reactive compassion	Responsive presence
"Reading" people's feelings	Sensing the collective dynamics
Surface-level sympathy	Deep structural awareness
Often leads to overwhelm	Sustainable and grounding
Tries to fix emotional states	Holds space for what emerges
Individual focus	Systems perspective
Can create codependency	Maintains healthy boundaries

Einfühlung is a more mature, grounded form of empathic engagement, one that allows leaders to feel deeply into organizational dynamics without becoming overwhelmed by them. The distinction between classic empathy and Einfühlung builds on historical notions of "feeling into" (Stein, 1989) and modern emotional intelligence research. Classic empathy centers on individual emotions, while Einfühlung extends to sensing organizational currents, similar to the empathy and organizational awareness competencies of emotional intelligence (Goleman & Boyatzis, 2017). This capacity emerges naturally from presence because when you're truly grounded and available, you can sense what's happening around you without losing yourself in it.

The Human Engine framework (sense, discern, imagine, respond, replenish) provides the operating system for translating Einfühlung into leadership practice. Each element represents both an inner capacity and an outer expression, creating a bridge between empathic awareness and effective action.

10.3 The Five Dimensions of Empathic Leadership

SENSE: LEADERSHIP AS ORGANIZATIONAL RADAR

The Practice: Present leaders become organizational radar systems, detecting subtle signals that traditional metrics miss. This isn't passive observation but active sensing that tunes into the emotional, relational, and energetic patterns that reveal organizational health.

What It Looks Like:
- Walking through work spaces and noticing shifts in energy, conversation patterns, and body language
- Sensing when meetings have unspoken tensions or unexpressed excitement
- Detecting early warning signals of burnout, disengagement, or emerging conflicts
- Feeling into whether decisions are landing well or creating resistance
- Picking up on cultural shifts before they become explicit

David Peters learned this the hard way. For months, his sensing capacity had been limited to financial dashboards and formal reports. He missed the gradual shift in team energy, the way conversations became more guarded, the subtle signs that people were running beyond capacity. When leaders don't sense well, they end up managing symptoms instead of addressing root causes.

Common Sensing Blind Spots:
- Getting lost in data while missing human dynamics
- Focusing only on explicit communication while ignoring emotional undertones

- Staying in executive suites instead of sensing what's happening throughout the organization
- Rushing through interactions without creating space to feel what's really happening

Sensing Across Diversity: Aisha Khan, a project manager in a multinational tech firm, noticed unease during a virtual team meeting with members from India, Germany, and the U.S. Despite positive project updates, the chat was quiet, and body language seemed reserved. Instead of moving to the agenda, Aisha paused and said, "I'm sensing some hesitation. Can we share what's on our minds, even if it's small?" After a moment, Priya from the India team shared concerns about unrealistic deadlines, which others echoed, revealing cultural differences in expressing dissent. Aisha facilitated a discussion to adjust timelines, ensuring all voices shaped the outcome. Her presence and inclusive sensing transformed a routine meeting into a trust-building moment, demonstrating Einfühlung across diverse perspectives.

Aisha's approach exemplifies how leaders can counteract power imbalances by creating space for marginalized or quieter voices, ensuring sensing reflects the full organizational field.

Developing Your Sensing Capacity:

Daily Practice: Start each day with a "sensing intention." Before checking email or diving into tasks, spend two minutes asking: "What do I most need to sense about my organization today?" This primes your awareness to notice relevant patterns.

Weekly Practice: Schedule "sensing walks" through different parts of your organization. Let your only agenda be to notice. What's the energy like? How are people interacting? What patterns do you observe? Keep a sensing journal to track patterns over time.

Meeting Practice: Before speaking in meetings, take 30 seconds to sense the room. What's the emotional tone? Where is there energy and where is there flatness? What wants to be said but hasn't been expressed yet?

DISCERN: LEADERSHIP AS MEANING-MAKING

The Practice: Discernment turns raw sensing into usable wisdom. It's the capacity to distinguish between surface phenomena and deeper patterns, between urgent noise and important signals, between what's symptomatic and what's systemic.

What It Looks Like:
- Recognizing when team conflicts are really about unclear expectations rather than personality clashes
- Distinguishing between creative tension (productive) and destructive tension (harmful)
- Knowing when resistance to change reflects legitimate concerns versus fear of the unknown
- Sensing when to push through challenges versus when to slow down and address underlying issues
- Discerning which problems need immediate attention versus which need time to ripen

The Discernment Challenge: In our information-saturated world, leaders often have too much data and too little wisdom. Discernment isn't about having more information but about developing the capacity to feel into what matters most in any given moment.

Common Discernment Traps:

- Treating all problems as urgent when some need patience to resolve
- Focusing on the loudest voices rather than sensing what the whole system needs
- Making decisions based on past patterns without sensing current reality
- Mistaking your personal emotion for collective reality

A Discernment Framework: To transform sensing into actionable wisdom, leaders can use the SIFT model (Sense, Integrate, Filter, Test). Sense the emotional and relational dynamics alongside data; Integrate diverse stakeholder perspectives; Filter out urgent noise to focus on systemic patterns; and Test insights through dialogue or small experiments before acting. This framework ensures discernment aligns with Einfühlung by grounding decisions in collective wisdom rather than reactive impulses.

SIFT Model:

- **Sense:** What do I sense about this situation (data, emotions, energy)?
- **Integrate:** What perspectives (team, stakeholders, diverse voices) inform my understanding?
- **Filter:** What's noise versus signal? What's symptomatic versus systemic?
- **Test:** How can I test my insight (e.g., pilot, dialogue) before committing?

Developing Your Discernment:

Decision Practice: Before making important decisions, create space for both analytical thinking and embodied sensing. Ask: "What does the data tell me?" Then ask: "What does my whole being sense about this situation?" Notice when these sources of information align and when they diverge.

Pattern Recognition: Keep a weekly reflection practice where you ask: "What patterns am I noticing in our organizational life? What wants my attention? What's trying to emerge that I haven't fully grasped yet?"

Consultation Practice: Regularly seek perspectives from people who sense differently than you do. Ask them not just what they think, but what they sense, feel, and intuit about situations you're trying to understand.

IMAGINE: LEADERSHIP AS POSSIBILITY SENSING

The Practice: Imagination, in the context of Einfühlung, isn't fantasy but the capacity to sense emerging possibilities that aren't yet visible. It's feeling into what wants to emerge in your organization and helping others see possibilities they couldn't imagine on their own.

What It Looks Like:
- Sensing potential in people that they don't yet see in themselves
- Feeling into market opportunities or threats before they become obvious
- Imagining organizational structures or processes that could better serve everyone involved
- Helping teams imagine solutions that solve more than one problem at once
- Creating shared vision that emerges from collective sensing rather than individual projection

The Imagination Edge: In rapidly changing environments, the ability to sense emerging possibilities becomes a crucial competitive advantage. Leaders who can feel into what's trying to emerge can position their organizations proactively rather than reactively.

Common Imagination Limitations:
- Projecting your own desires rather than sensing what wants to emerge
- Getting attached to specific outcomes instead of staying open to possibilities
- Imagining from your head rather than from embodied sensing
- Creating visions that inspire you but don't resonate with others

Developing Your Imagination:

Future Sensing: Regularly spend time imagining your organization three years from now. But instead of strategic planning, try sensing into it. What does it feel like? What's the energy? How are people interacting? What's become possible?

Possibility Dialogues: Create conversations with your team where you collectively imagine ideal futures. Ask: "If we could create anything we wanted, what would our organization feel like? What would become possible for our people, our customers, our community?"

Edge Exploration: Identify the thresholds where your organization meets the unknown. Spend time sensing into these edges. What opportunities or challenges are emerging that you haven't fully recognized yet?

RESPOND: LEADERSHIP AS SKILLFUL ACTION

The Practice: Response, differentiated from reaction, is action that emerges from deep sensing, clear discernment, and expanded imagination. It's leadership that acts from understanding rather than urgency, from wisdom rather than habit.

What It Looks Like:
- Addressing underlying patterns rather than just surface symptoms
- Timing interventions based on organizational readiness rather than your own impatience
- Responding to what the system truly needs, not what you assume it should
- Taking action that serves the whole rather than just solving immediate problems
- Creating interventions that invite participation rather than demanding compliance

When David Peters responded to his sensing in that quarterly review, he didn't jump immediately to solutions. He created space for the truth to emerge, listened deeply to what his team was experiencing, and then worked with them to design responses that addressed root causes rather than symptoms.

The Response Discipline: The gap between sensing and responding is where wisdom lives. Leaders who respond skillfully have learned to pause, consult their deeper knowing, and choose actions that serve the larger good rather than just relieve immediate pressure.

Common Response Pitfalls:

- Reacting to symptoms rather than responding to root causes
- Taking action before fully understanding what's needed
- Imposing solutions rather than inviting collaborative responses
- Responding from your own emotions rather than from collective wisdom
- Acting too quickly or too slowly for what the situation requires

Developing Your Response Capacity:

Response Planning: Before key meetings or decisions, pause to sense: What kind of response does this moment call for? Is this a time for listening or action? For patience or urgency? For individual decision-making or collective deliberation?

Impact Sensing: After taking significant actions, regularly check in with affected stakeholders to sense how your response landed. What worked? What missed the mark? What can you learn about responding more skillfully?

Response Partners: Identify people who can help you sense whether your planned responses are wise. Before taking major actions, consult with people who can offer different perspectives on what the situation needs.

REPLENISH: LEADERSHIP AS SUSTAINABLE PRESENCE

The Practice: Replenishment ensures that your capacity for presence and Einfühlung remains sustainable over time. It's not just personal self-care but the discipline of maintaining the inner resources that make empathic leadership possible.

What It Looks Like:

- Recognizing when your sensing capacity is becoming depleted or distorted
- Creating rhythms that restore your ability to be present and feel into organizational dynamics
- Modeling sustainability as a shared responsibility
- Building systems that support collective replenishment rather than just individual recovery
- Maintaining practices that keep you grounded and centered even under pressure

The Sustainability Imperative: Leaders who don't replenish well eventually lose their capacity for accurate sensing, clear discernment, and wise response. They become reactive rather than responsive, mechanical rather than empathic, depleted rather than generative.

Common Depletion Patterns:

- Ignoring early signs of emotional or physical exhaustion
- Trying to maintain empathic leadership through willpower rather than sustainable practices
- Focusing on individual recovery while ignoring systemic sources of depletion
- Treating replenishment as optional rather than essential
- Burning out your empathic capacity by taking on others' emotions

Developing Your Replenishment Practice:

Daily Reset: Create transition rituals between different parts of your day. This might be three conscious breaths before entering meetings, a brief walk between appointments, or a moment of gratitude at the end of the workday.

Weekly Restoration: Schedule time for activities that restore your capacity for presence: time in nature, creative pursuits, meaningful conversations, or whatever helps you return to your center.

Systemic Sustainability: Look for ways to create organizational conditions that support everyone's capacity for presence and empathic engagement rather than depleting it.

10.4 Integrating the Five Dimensions

These five dimensions work together as an integrated system. Strong sensing informs wise discernment. Clear discernment expands imagination. Expanded imagination enables skillful response. And sustainable replenishment maintains your capacity for the entire cycle.

The key is starting where you are and building systematically. You don't need to master all five dimensions simultaneously. Begin with presence, the foundation that makes everything else possible. Then gradually develop your capacity in each dimension, noticing how they support and strengthen each other.

David Peters began with sensing: learning to notice what his previous focus on metrics had caused him to miss. As his sensing capacity developed, his discernment improved. He could distinguish between surface problems and deeper patterns. This led to expanded imagination about what was possible for his organization, more skillful responses to emerging challenges, and ultimately a more sustainable way of leading that served both performance and people.

10.5 Creating Organizational Einfühlung: The Cultural Cultivation Approach

When individual leaders develop these five dimensions, the impact extends far beyond their personal effectiveness.

173

Presence is contagious. As you model empathic leadership, others begin to develop their own capacity for sensing, discerning, imagining, responding, and replenishing.

But creating organizational Einfühlung isn't a change initiative but cultural cultivation. Unlike structural changes that can be implemented through policies and procedures, Einfühlung emerges through the gradual transformation of how people relate to each other and to the work itself. You feel these shifts long before you can measure them.

Over time, this creates organizational Einfühlung: a collective capacity to feel into shared experience and respond wisely. But this transformation happens organically, through modeling and influence rather than mandate and metrics.

The Long Game of Cultural Change

Developing organizational Einfühlung requires a fundamentally different approach to leadership, one focused on being rather than doing, on influence rather than control, on cultivation rather than implementation.

Start Where You Are: The journey begins with your own practice. You can't cultivate organizational sensing capacity without first developing your own ability to sense, discern, imagine, respond, and replenish. As your presence becomes more grounded and your empathic capacity deepens, people around you begin to feel the difference.

Work in Pockets: Rather than trying to transform the entire organization at once, focus on your immediate sphere of influence. Create conditions within your team where authentic sensing and honest communication become natural. These pockets of empathic culture become demonstration sites that others can observe and eventually adopt.

Trust the Ripple Effect: Empathic leadership spreads through relationship and example rather than training programs. When people experience what it feels like to be truly seen and heard, to have their sensing valued, to be part of collective discernment, they begin to offer the same quality of presence to others.

Measure What Emerges: Traditional metrics often miss the early signs of cultural transformation. Instead of looking for immediate behavioral changes, watch for subtle signs: more honest conversations, people feeling safer to voice concerns, teams naturally pausing to sense before major decisions, conflicts being met with curiosity rather than defensiveness.

The Organic Indicators of Transformation

You feel organizational Einfühlung developing long before any survey can measure it:

In the Quality of Silence: Meetings develop a different rhythm. Instead of rushing to fill every pause, teams become comfortable with moments of collective sensing. Silence becomes fertile rather than awkward.

In How Conflict Shows Up: Disagreements shift from positional arguing to collaborative sensing into what the situation actually needs. Resistance is met with curiosity: "What is this resistance trying to protect?"

In the Speed of Trust: Information flows more freely because people sense that their contributions will be received with genuine consideration rather than judgment or dismissal.

In Collective Intuition: Teams begin to sense emerging patterns (market shifts, customer needs, internal tensions) before data confirms what they're feeling.

In Sustainable Pace: The organization naturally develops rhythms that honor both productivity and renewal, not because policies mandate it but because the culture has developed sensitivity to collective energy and capacity.

10.6 The Neuroscience of Empathic Leadership

Recent advances in neuroscience help us understand why presence-based leadership has such a profound impact on organizational dynamics. When you're truly present with others, your nervous systems actually begin to synchronize (Porges, 2011). This isn't metaphorical; it's measurable through heart rate variability, brain wave patterns, and stress hormone levels.

Your presence as a leader functions as a co-regulating influence on the nervous systems of those around you. When you're centered, calm, and present, you create a field of regulation that helps others access their own capacity for clear thinking, creative problem-solving, and authentic communication. This co-regulation is further supported by research on neural synchrony, which shows that a leader's calm presence can reduce team stress responses, fostering collective problem-solving (Hasson et al., 2012).

Mirror neurons help explain how emotional states spread between people (Gallese & Goldman, 1998). But Einfühlung involves more than just emotional contagion. It requires embodied simulation: the ability to internally simulate another person's experience while maintaining awareness of your own state. Presence-based leadership aligns with neural integration, enabling leaders to attune to others' experiences while maintaining self-awareness (Siegel, 2010).

This neurobiological understanding validates what contemplative traditions have known for millennia: the quality of your presence directly affects the capacity of those around you. When you develop your ability to sense, discern, imagine, respond, and replenish from a place of grounded presence, you create conditions where others can access these same capacities.

Practical Neuroscience: This isn't just theoretical—it has immediate implications for daily leadership practice. Your morning presence practice doesn't just center you; it creates a field of regulation that your team can feel. A simple 30-second pause can shift the nervous system of an entire room. The sustainable replenishment you model gives others permission to restore rather than deplete themselves.

10.7 Your Leadership Practice: Getting Started

The transformation from traditional leadership to empathic leadership begins with small, consistent practices. Here's how to start:

Week 1: Foundation Building
- Begin each day with two minutes of presence practice: simply sensing your body, breath, and immediate environment
- In meetings, practice taking 30 seconds to sense the room before speaking
- End each day by reflecting: "What did I sense today that I might normally have missed?"

Week 2: Expanding Sensing
- Add a weekly "sensing walk" through your organization
- Practice asking "What else wants to be said here?" in conversations
- Begin keeping a brief sensing journal to track patterns

Week 3: Developing Discernment

- Before making decisions, ask both "What does the data tell me?" and "What does my whole being sense?"
- Practice distinguishing between urgent and important
- Seek perspectives from people who sense differently than you do

Week 4: Cultivating Imagination

- Spend time imagining your organization's ideal future from an embodied rather than analytical perspective
- Create possibility dialogues with your team
- Explore the edges where your organization meets the unknown

Month 2 and Beyond:

- Integrate response practices that serve the whole system
- Develop sustainable replenishment routines
- Begin modeling these practices for others

10.8 The Ripple Effects of Empathic Leadership

The journey from traditional leadership to empathic leadership is ultimately a journey from isolation to connection, from reaction to response, from control to influence, from depletion to regeneration. When you develop your capacity for Einfühlung— for feeling into the organizational life around you—you don't just become a more effective leader. You become a catalyst for organizational transformation.

Your presence becomes a gift to everyone whose life your leadership touches. The quality of attention you bring to meetings, the depth of listening you offer in conversations, the space you create for truth to emerge: these seemingly small acts create ripples that extend far beyond what you can see.

As you develop your capacity to sense, discern, imagine, respond, and replenish from a place of grounded presence, you discover that empathic leadership isn't just a nice way to lead but a more intelligent way to lead. You make better decisions because you're working with more complete information. You create more sustainable solutions because you're addressing root causes rather than symptoms. You inspire greater commitment because people feel truly seen and heard.

But perhaps most importantly, you model a way of being that gives others permission to bring their full humanity to work. In a world that often demands we fragment ourselves—leaving our emotions at home, our bodies at the door, our deeper wisdom in the parking lot—empathic leadership creates space for wholeness.

This is the foundation for organizational Einfühlung: leaders who have learned to feel into the deeper currents of organizational life and respond from that place of understanding. It begins with your presence, extends through your practice, and ultimately transforms the very culture in which you lead.

The five dimensions (sense, discern, imagine, respond, replenish) provide both a framework for development and a reminder that empathic leadership is not a destination but a practice. Each day offers new opportunities to sense more clearly, discern more wisely, imagine more boldly, respond more skillfully, and replenish more sustainably.

Your organization—and the world beyond—awaits this kind of leadership. The people you serve, the colleagues you work with, and the communities you impact hunger for leaders who can feel into what's really happening and respond with wisdom. By practicing Einfühlung, you not only transform your organization but also contribute to broader systemic change—whether by fostering equitable workplaces, advancing environmental sustainability, or rebuilding trust in fractured societies. Commit to this practice daily, knowing your presence can spark ripples that reshape not just your team but the larger systems you touch. The choice to lead with Einfühlung is yours, and its impact extends far beyond what you can imagine.

The question isn't whether you can lead this way—but whether you'll choose to. The choice is yours, and the impact extends far beyond what you might imagine.

10.9 Your Five-Dimension Practice

Daily (5 minutes):
- **Sense:** Start with presence. What do I need to sense today?
- **Discern:** In decisions, consult both analysis and embodied wisdom. Apply one SIFT step to a decision today, noting systemic versus surface issues.
- **Imagine:** Stay open to possibilities beyond current constraints
- **Respond:** Act from understanding rather than urgency
- **Replenish:** Create transitions that restore rather than deplete

Weekly (30 minutes):
- Sensing walk through your organization
- Reflection: What patterns am I noticing?
- Possibility dialogue with team members
- Response review: How did my actions land?
- Replenishment check: What do I need to sustain this practice?

Monthly (2 hours):

- Deep sensing into organizational health and emerging needs
- Consultation with diverse perspectives on what you're noticing
- Imagination session: What wants to emerge in our organization?
- Response planning: How can we serve what's trying to emerge?
- Systemic replenishment: How can we create more sustainable conditions for everyone?
- Systemic Impact: Reflect on how your leadership can address a broader societal challenge (e.g., equity, sustainability)

Remember: This isn't one more thing for your to-do list—it's how the list becomes more human.

The Human Engine isn't machinery—it's a living rhythm.

Chapter 11

WHEN SYSTEMS PUSH BACK

Resistance as a Form of Intelligence

"You never change things by fighting the existing reality. To change something, build a new model that makes the old model obsolete."
—Buckminster Fuller

As you cultivate the Human Engine of sensing, discerning, imagining, responding, and replenishing, you begin to notice what others miss. You sense burnout before it hits the dashboard. You feel when a strategy isn't resonating before it unravels. You detect unseen opportunities and resistance not by data, but by energy, by mood, silence, and shift.

But here's the paradox: the more deeply you feel into the system, the more likely it is to push back.

Organizations designed for control and predictability often reject the very intelligence that could help them evolve. They treat sensing as threat, attunement as interference, and vulnerability as risk. The immune system of the status quo kicks in, not because the system is broken, but because it's protecting what it was built to preserve.

This chapter is about navigating that resistance, not as an obstacle to overcome, but as intelligence to listen to. If we want to help systems evolve, we must learn to meet resistance not with force, but with design. Not with judgment, but with deeper discernment. We must build new models, not just argue with old ones.

The Illusion of Frictionless Change

Maya Chen stared at the email, her stomach tightening. As Chief People Officer at Meridian Healthcare, she had spent six months championing culture transformation: psychological safety, authentic connection, collaborative innovation. The initiative had launched with genuine enthusiasm—leadership retreats practicing vulnerability, training on constructive feedback, redesigned meeting protocols.

Yet participation in her peer coaching circles was declining steadily. Team leaders reported being "too busy with real work" to engage. Even enthusiastic early adopters were finding reasons to step back.

No one was openly opposing her efforts. Instead, resistance manifested as collective drift—a silent, steady migration back to familiar patterns despite apparent commitment to change.

"What am I missing?" Maya wondered. She had secured the CEO's backing, created a compelling vision based on solid research, designed thoughtful implementation steps, and communicated persistently. She had followed every principle from the change management playbook. Why wasn't it working?

Maya was encountering a truth every change agent discovers: systems push back through complex, interconnected mechanisms designed to maintain existing order. This resistance is fundamental to how systems preserve their identity.

The prevailing narrative treats organizational resistance as something to "overcome" through better change management. This misses a profound truth: resistance contains wisdom about the system that change agents need to understand.

This chapter offers a contrarian view: resistance as intelligence to listen to. Rather than seeing it as an enemy to be conquered, we'll explore it as a teacher that reveals hidden system dynamics, a guardian that protects essential functions, and a partner in co-creating sustainable transformation.

The journey begins not with techniques for overcoming resistance, but with a deeper understanding of why systems push back, and what this resistance has to teach us about creating change that endures.

11.1 Recognizing Resistance as System Intelligence

When Resistance Speaks: Decoding the System's Intelligence

The peer coaching circles were failing not because people didn't value connection, but because the electronic medical record system required such meticulous documentation that clinicians worked through lunches and stayed late—precisely when coaching circles were scheduled. New meeting protocols encouraging diverse voices were undermined by performance metrics rewarding individual achievement. Vulnerability embraced in leadership retreats couldn't survive a policy environment where mistakes triggered lengthy incident reports.

The resistance wasn't personal; it was systemic.

The conventional approach focuses heavily on individual psychology, treating "resistance to change" as personal failing. This person-centered view misunderstands organizations as complex systems. As family systems therapist Virginia Satir observed, "The problem is not the problem; coping is the problem." Resistant individuals often reflect the system's established patterns for maintaining stability.

Consider a healthcare organization that attempted to implement more holistic, patient-centered care. Individual physicians expressed skepticism and resistance, which change leaders initially attributed to professional stubbornness or fear of change. Deeper investigation revealed that the electronic medical record system made holistic care nearly impossible by fragmenting patient information across multiple screens and prioritizing billing codes over narratives. The physicians' resistance wasn't personal opposition to patient-centered care; it was an accurate reading of systemic constraints.

The Organizational Immune System

Organizations develop invisible grammars: unwritten rules governing what's possible and prohibited (Bateson, 1972). These rules, embedded in structures, processes, and norms, shape behavior more powerfully than any mission statement.

The most powerful form of systemic resistance is homeostasis: living systems' tendency to maintain internal stability by resisting change. Organizations possess immune-like mechanisms that protect against perceived threats, often so subtly we misattribute their effects to individual choices.

When leaders introduce practices that violate the system's grammar, such as vulnerability in a culture of stoic professionalism, or collaboration in structures that reward individual achievement, the organization responds not through conscious conspiracy but through its embedded logic. Meeting agendas mysteriously fill with urgent matters, leaving no time for new practices. Budgets tighten precisely when resources would be needed for change initiatives. Career advancement subtly favors those who maintain traditional approaches over those championing new directions.

Resistance as Intelligence, Not Opposition

Systems theorist Barry Oshry argues that resistance often signals legitimate concerns: "Resistance is feedback. There is intelligence in it that we need to understand." When nurses resist an efficiency initiative that reduces patient time, they're protecting the essence of caregiving itself.

This shifts our orientation. Instead of treating pushback as an obstacle, it becomes data: intelligence about the system that can inform more sustainable change. The question changes from "How do we overcome resistance?" to "What is this resistance telling us?"

Effective change requires systemic intervention: work that addresses the grammar of the system itself. This begins with making the system visible to itself—"seeing our seeing"—making explicit the implicit rules and patterns governing organizational behavior (Scharmer, 2009).

When a financial services firm struggled to implement a more collaborative approach to client relationships, the breakthrough came not through more persuasive communication or stronger incentives. Instead, leaders convened a series of "system seeing" sessions where cross-functional teams mapped the invisible forces shaping current behavior, from compensation systems to meeting structures to unspoken status hierarchies. This collective seeing made previously invisible patterns discussable, opening possibilities for coordinated shifts in multiple dimensions simultaneously.

The Resistance Decoder Map

When encountering resistance to change, use these questions to decode its systemic intelligence:

1. **What is being protected?** What core functions, values, or identities might be threatened by the proposed change?
2. **What contradictions exist?** Where do formal structures, incentives, or processes directly undermine the desired change?
3. **What remains invisible?** What assumptions, norms, or power dynamics operate below conscious awareness?
4. **What legitimate concerns are hidden within the resistance?** What risks or losses might the system be accurately perceiving?
5. **What deeper alignment is possible?** How might the change be redesigned to work with rather than against the system's core purpose?

Use this map not just individually but collectively, and invite those expressing resistance to explore these questions together, creating shared understanding of systemic dynamics.

The wisdom in this approach is simple but powerful: meaningful change doesn't happen by overpowering resistance. It comes from engaging with it: listening for the intelligence it carries about the system. The resistant middle manager isn't merely an obstacle, but a sensor revealing where the change effort may be overlooking crucial realities. The skeptical frontline worker isn't simply afraid of change, but often pointing toward legitimate concerns about how abstract visions will impact concrete daily work.

For Maya at Meridian Healthcare, this reframing led to a breakthrough. Rather than trying harder to persuade people to participate in coaching circles, she began investigating what the resistance was revealing. Through candid conversations with clinicians, she discovered that the initiative wasn't failing because people didn't value connection; it was failing because the operational reality made participation nearly impossible.

This insight shifted her approach entirely. She began collaborating with operations and IT leaders to identify how electronic documentation requirements could be streamlined. She worked with schedulers to protect specific times for developmental activities. She engaged finance to revise performance metrics to include collaborative outcomes. Rather than fighting resistance, she let it guide her toward a more integrated approach to change.

11.2 Cultural Sensing in Diverse Systems

Maya stared at the participation data from her peer coaching circles, puzzled by an unexpected pattern. The circles in the Emergency Department were thriving, with deep engagement and measurable improvements in team cohesion. But the circles in Cardiology, despite having equally committed leadership and similar operational pressures, were struggling with polite disengagement. People attended, nodded thoughtfully, but rarely shared authentically.

During a candid conversation with Dr. Patel, the Cardiology department head, a different picture emerged. "The concept is sound," he said carefully, "but many of our physicians come from cultures where sharing personal struggles with peers, especially across hierarchical lines, requires a different approach. They've adapted beautifully to American medical practice, but asking a senior attending to be vulnerable in front of residents still triggers deep cultural programming about respect and face."

Dr. Patel continued: "And our nursing staff, many from the Philippines, are incredibly empathetic, but they're waiting for different signals about group safety. In their cultural framework, individual psychological safety comes after collective harmony is established. They need to sense that the whole group is aligned before any individual risks openness."

This conversation illuminated one of the most nuanced aspects of systemic empathy: even in organizations where people have successfully acculturated to American professional norms, deeper cultural patterns continue to shape how empathy is experienced, expressed, and received.

Beyond Surface Acculturation

Research on cultural adaptation reveals a crucial distinction between behavioral acculturation and deeper value persistence. While professionals from diverse cultural backgrounds quickly master American organizational behaviors, their underlying frameworks for relationship, hierarchy, and emotional expression often retain strong cultural influences.

Empathy may be universal in capacity, but it is profoundly cultural in expression. Research analyzing responses from over 100,000 participants across 63 countries found significant variation in how empathy is experienced and displayed (Chopik et al., 2017).

In cultures with interdependent self-construals, empathy is often enacted through role-appropriate behavior, group attunement, and respectful silence rather than verbal vulnerability or direct feedback (Markus & Kitayama, 1991).

Think of Filipino nurses who waited until group harmony was established before opening up individually, or physicians from hierarchical cultures who could give technical feedback upward but felt sharing personal struggles with supervisors was culturally inappropriate. What appears as resistance is often culturally grounded relational intelligence: efforts to preserve harmony, respect hierarchy, or protect collective identity.

Research across over 70 countries identified key cultural dimensions: power distance (how societies handle power differences), individualism versus collectivism, uncertainty avoidance, and long-term versus short-term orientation (Hofstede, 2001). While some behaviors adapt quickly in organizational contexts, individualism versus collectivism and temporal orientation appear to have deeper roots, persisting even among highly acculturated professionals.

For empathic leaders, this creates both opportunity and complexity. The opportunity lies in accessing diverse forms of emotional intelligence and sensing capabilities that different cultural backgrounds bring. The complexity emerges when well-intentioned empathic practices inadvertently privilege one cultural style of connection over others.

When Cultural Programming Blocks System Intelligence

Maya's cultural awareness was deepened by a conversation with David, a consultant who had worked extensively in South Asia. He shared a striking example from his time at a nonprofit in India that provided workshop opportunities for people with disabilities.

"I kept encountering this pattern," David explained. "During our quality review meetings, when I'd ask if there were any problems with the production process, everyone would nod and say everything was fine. But privately, I'd discover significant quality issues that workers had noticed but never reported. The polite thing, the culturally appropriate thing, was to instinctively agree with the person in authority. Never raise objections, never challenge."

David's breakthrough came when he realized this wasn't resistance to improvement but adherence to cultural values around respect and hierarchy. "I had to completely reframe the work. Before we could implement any production improvements, we had to help the team learn how to say 'no.' Not to be oppositional, but because 'no' was the first step in raising objections, highlighting quality problems, and creating the feedback loops we needed."

Cultural programming around power distance doesn't just affect emotional vulnerability—it can block the very information flows that organizations need to sense problems and improve performance.

The Empathic Authority Paradox

David's experience revealed the empathic authority paradox. In cultures with strong interdependent self-construals, the desire to show respect and maintain harmony can actually prevent the authentic communication that empathic leaders most need to hear. Team members may:

- Agree with initiatives they have concerns about
- Avoid surfacing operational problems to "protect" leadership from bad news
- Interpret requests for honest feedback as tests of loyalty rather than genuine invitations
- Express disagreement indirectly through reduced engagement rather than direct communication

The irony is that this cultural courtesy, intended to maintain relationship, can actually undermine the deeper connections that empathic leadership seeks to create.

Cultural Undercurrents in Empathic Practice

Maya began to notice how these persistent cultural patterns manifested in seemingly universal empathic practices:

Collectivist Sensing: Team members from collectivist cultures often read group dynamics sophisticatedly but express concern differently—reducing engagement until group harmony is restored rather than voicing individual complaints.

Hierarchical Vulnerability: Professionals from high-power distance cultures could collaborate across levels but sharing personal struggles with supervisors felt culturally inappropriate.

Temporal Expectations: Some expected longer relationship-building phases before authentic sharing; others grew impatient with gradual trust-building.

Expression Styles: While some cultures value direct emotional expression, others demonstrate care through consistent presence, practical support, or respectful attention.

Reframing Authority for Cultural Safety

Maya learned to distinguish between cultural resistance and cultural navigation. When team members from cultures emphasizing interdependent self-construals seemed overly agreeable, she began asking herself: "Are they resisting empathic leadership, or are they practicing it within their cultural framework of respect and relational harmony?" This reframing helped her understand that deference to authority or indirect communication wasn't resistance but an alternate cultural grammar of respect and care.

This reframing led to practical adjustments:

Permission Structures: Rather than simply asking "Any concerns?" Maya learned to create explicit permission for disagreement: "I need to hear what's not working, even if it's uncomfortable to say. Your willingness to tell me hard truths is how you help me be a better leader."

Indirect Feedback Channels: She created anonymous suggestion systems and used trusted intermediaries to gather concerns that might not surface in direct supervisor conversations.

Modeling Vulnerability First: Before asking for feedback, Maya would share her own uncertainties and mistakes, demonstrating that admitting problems was not disrespectful but helpful.

Cultural Reframing: She learned to position feedback-giving as an act of service and respect rather than challenge to authority: "Your insights help me serve our patients better" rather than "I need you to be more honest with me."

The Cultural Intelligence Expansion

Recognizing these patterns, Maya developed cultural sensing: the ability to detect how cultural undercurrents shaped empathic dynamics even in acculturated teams. This involved several key capabilities:

Pattern Recognition: Learning to distinguish between individual resistance and cultural navigation. When multiple team members from similar cultural backgrounds responded similarly to empathic practices, this suggested cultural rather than personal factors.

Adaptive Framing: Presenting the same empathic principles through different cultural lenses. Psychological safety for individualist team members versus collective strength for collectivist members. Personal growth for short-term orientation versus sustained team development for long-term orientation.

Multiple Pathways: Creating different routes to the same empathic outcomes. Some team members connected through one-on-one conversations, others through group processes, still others through shared work rather than explicit emotional sharing.

Practical Integration: The Cultural Empathy Audit

Maya developed a simple but powerful tool for leaders navigating multicultural empathic dynamics:

Before implementing empathic practices, consider:

1. **Cultural Composition:** What cultural backgrounds are represented on your team? Which Hofstede dimensions might be most relevant?
2. **Acculturation Variations:** How long have team members been in American organizational contexts? What levels of cultural adaptation might coexist?
3. **Empathy Expression Preferences:** How do different cultural groups on your team naturally express care, concern, and connection?
4. **Hierarchy Comfort:** What cultural programming around power distance might affect cross-level vulnerability and feedback?
5. **Group vs. Individual Focus:** Which team members might prioritize collective harmony before individual expression?

During empathic practices, ask:

- "How might someone from [X cultural background] experience this differently?"
- "What would make this feel culturally safe for everyone?"
- "Are we inadvertently privileging one cultural style of empathy?"
- "What different pathways could achieve the same empathic outcomes?"

Integration Without Stereotyping

The goal wasn't to create cultural boxes or assume uniform responses within cultural groups. Rather, Maya learned to hold cultural awareness lightly as one lens among many for understanding system dynamics. Some individuals had moved far from their cultural origins, others retained strong connections, and most existed somewhere in between.

The key insight was recognizing that resistance to empathic practices might reflect cultural intelligence rather than opposition to empathy itself. When team members seemed disengaged from vulnerability-based practices, they might be signaling that empathy needed different pathways in their cultural framework.

The Breakthrough: Multicultural Empathic Design

Maya's breakthrough came when she stopped trying to overcome cultural differences and started designing with them. She created multiple pathways to the same empathic outcomes:

- Group sensing circles for collectivist-oriented team members
- Structured reflection processes that honored hierarchical sensitivity
- Extended relationship-building phases for long-term orientation preferences
- Action-based connection for cultures emphasizing practical care over verbal sharing

The result wasn't cultural accommodation, but cultural integration: leveraging diverse empathic intelligences to create stronger, more resilient team connections. The Emergency Department's success hadn't come from cultural homogeneity but from accidentally creating pathways that worked across cultural styles. Cardiology's struggles reflected not cultural barriers but design limitations.

Expanding System Intelligence

This cultural dimension added richness to Maya's understanding of resistance as system intelligence. Sometimes resistance contained not just organizational wisdom but cultural wisdom: insights about different ways humans create safety, express care, and build authentic connection.

The multicultural team became not a complication for empathic leadership but an asset, offering diverse sensing capabilities and multiple pathways to the human connections that drove both wellbeing and performance. The challenge wasn't overcoming cultural differences but orchestrating them into a more complete empathic system.

As Maya reflected months later, "I thought I was implementing universal empathic practices. I discovered that empathy itself is universal, but its expressions are beautifully diverse. The system's resistance was teaching me to become a more culturally intelligent empathic leader."

This cultural intelligence would prove essential as Maya's work expanded beyond individual teams to organization-wide transformation, where cultural diversity became not an obstacle to navigate but a resource to leverage in creating more human, more effective organizational cultures.

Understanding these cultural undercurrents in empathic practice prepared Maya for another systemic challenge: the persistent organizational belief that human connection and operational efficiency exist in fundamental tension.

11.3 Beyond the Fix-It Reflex

The Fix-It Mentality

The conventional response to organizational challenges follows a predictable pattern: identify the problem, design a solution, implement the fix. This mechanistic approach assumes that organizations operate like machines: input the right intervention, and get the desired output. But the very framework of "fixing" can become part of the problem.

Human vs. Efficient: A False Tradeoff

As Maya continued her cultural transformation work at Meridian, she encountered another form of systemic resistance: the persistent belief that focusing on human connection would undermine operational efficiency. When proposing changes to meeting structures that would create space for more meaningful dialogue, she heard comments like: "That sounds nice in theory, but we need to maintain productivity" or "We just don't have time for the soft stuff when we're facing these performance targets."

This resistance revealed the most pernicious false dichotomy in organizational life: the supposed tradeoff between efficiency and humanity. This artificial opposition frames organizational design as a zero-sum game: we can have systems that maximize productivity and profit, or we can have workplaces that honor human dignity and potential, but not both.

This dichotomy pervades management thinking: "hard" business imperatives versus "soft" human concerns, "performance management" versus "employee wellbeing," "running a tight ship" versus "creating a supportive culture." Yet this framing misunderstands both efficiency and humanity. The most efficient organizations might be precisely those that most fully honor human potential.

The modern organization was conceived during the industrial revolution, modeled explicitly on the machine. Frederick Taylor's "scientific management" sought to engineer human work with the same principles used to optimize mechanical processes: standardization, specialization, and control.

This mechanistic paradigm views the human as a component, a resource to be utilized efficiently, rather than a living being with intrinsic value and potential. What began as a metaphor gradually hardened into structures, processes, and cultural assumptions that treat people as interchangeable parts.

This paradigm creates I-It relationships: instrumental connections where one treats the other as an object to be used rather than a subject to be encountered (Buber, 1970). Such relationships may produce compliance, but never unleash the full creative potential that emerges from genuine human connection.

When Humanity Drives Performance

A growing body of evidence demonstrates that the most demonstrably efficient organizations are precisely those that most fully honor human dignity and potential. These organizations transcend the false dichotomy to achieve "humanistic efficiency": performance that flows from rather than against human nature.

Consider Buurtzorg, a Dutch home healthcare provider that replaced hierarchical management with self-organizing nurse teams, achieving 40% lower cost per patient and 50% less required care hours with better outcomes. Or Southwest Airlines, which built the most financially successful airline in history on employee empowerment and authentic human connection.

How do humanistic organizations achieve this integration? Rather than fragmenting work into disconnected tasks, they design roles that engage the whole person and connect directly to purpose. Rather than controlling through elaborate monitoring systems, they create conditions of trust that simultaneously reduce bureaucratic overhead and unleash discretionary effort. Rather than relying on external incentives, they cultivate authentic connection to purpose that generates intrinsic motivation.

For Maya at Meridian Healthcare, this understanding provided a powerful reframing. Rather than positioning culture change as a "soft" initiative competing with "hard" operational imperatives, she began documenting how human disconnection was directly undermining efficiency: communication breakdowns that delayed care, burnout that increased costly turnover, and trust deficits that prevented problem-solving collaboration.

Armed with this analysis, she built partnerships with operations and finance leaders to identify integration points where human connection directly enhanced operational performance. They redesigned bed transition processes to include brief relationship-building conversations between shifts, adding just two minutes to handoffs but reducing medication errors by 23%. They restructured team meetings to begin with personal check-ins. This initially seemed inefficient, but ultimately shortened meeting times by creating psychological safety for direct communication about operational challenges.

11.4 Dancing with Tension, Not Controlling It

The System's Gravitational Field: Understanding Institutional Inertia

Six months into her revised approach, Maya was seeing promising signs. The integrated changes addressed both cultural and operational dimensions simultaneously and were gaining traction across several departments. Yet she remained puzzled by the uneven adoption. Why were some areas embracing the new approaches while others maintained business as usual despite similar exposure to the same initiatives?

The answer emerged through conversations with Meridian's longest-serving employees. They pointed to historical patterns that helped explain the present resistance. Departments that had previously experienced failed change initiatives were most skeptical. Areas that had suffered budget cuts following past "efficiency" programs interpreted Maya's work through that lens, despite her different approach. Units with long-serving leaders who had risen through Meridian's traditional command-and-control culture subtly reinforced those norms even while verbally supporting the new direction.

Maya was encountering institutional inertia: the tendency of established systems to maintain familiar patterns despite changing conditions or explicit intentions to change. This emerges from interlocking structures, processes, and cultural elements designed to ensure organizational stability.

The physical organization of work—buildings, departments, reporting lines, job descriptions—literally embodies the current order. As architect Winston Churchill observed, "We shape our buildings, and afterwards our buildings shape us." A financial services firm discovered this truth when attempting to foster more collaborative work within a physical environment of private offices and hierarchical executive floors. The architecture itself silently reinforced the very patterns they hoped to change.

Beyond physical structure lies organizational routines: standard operating procedures that become automatic and invisible over time, functioning as "organizational memory" that preserves institutional patterns (March & Simon, 1958). Perhaps most powerful is organizational culture: shared assumptions, values, and norms that continuously reproduce themselves and shape what members can and cannot see.

These interlocking structures, routines, and norms create "interdependent behaviors": patterns ˙ that quietly resist piecemeal change (Weick, 1979). When everything connects to everything else, changing any single element triggers compensating adjustments that restore the original pattern.

From Naive to Strategic Intervention

Confronted with institutional inertia, many leaders resort to naive interventions: believing inspiration alone will overcome systemic constraints, assuming structural change will automatically produce new behaviors, or expecting procedural adjustments to shift deeply embedded patterns.

These approaches share a mechanistic understanding of organizations, systematically underestimating both system complexity and the emergent nature of meaningful change.

A more sophisticated approach recognizes institutional inertia not as an enemy to be conquered but as a reality to be worked with. This orientation shifts from controlling the system to influencing its evolution by activating constructive constraints: conditions that simultaneously limit and enable new possibilities.

Rather than focusing on single points of leverage, effective change involves coordinated shifts across multiple dimensions. When a manufacturing company simultaneously reorganized teams, redesigned layouts, changed metrics, and created new symbols of collaboration, meaningful transformation became possible.

While revolutionary rhetoric often accompanies change initiatives, lasting transformation typically happens through "gradual radicalism": cumulative shifts that respect the system's need for coherence while steadily moving toward fundamentally new patterns. This approach maintains integration while avoiding the immune response triggered by perceived threats to identity.

For Maya at Meridian, this understanding led to a more ecological approach to change. Rather than pushing equally hard across all departments, she began working with variation, identifying areas of the organization where conditions were more favorable for culture change and investing disproportionate energy there. These "microcultures of possibility" became demonstration sites where others could witness the integrated approach in action.

She also became more deliberate about pacing, recognizing that institutional inertia couldn't be overcome through sheer force of will. She identified key leverage points: moments like leadership transitions, technology implementations, or physical space renovations where multiple dimensions could shift simultaneously. She created scaffolding: temporary structures that supported new behaviors until they could become self-sustaining.

In-the-Moment Resistance Practice

When you encounter pushback in real time, try this simple practice:

1. **Pause (10 seconds):** Before defending or pushing harder, take a breath and notice your own reaction to the resistance.
2. **Listen for Intelligence (30 seconds):** Ask yourself: "What might this resistance be trying to protect or preserve? What legitimate concern might be hidden here?"
3. **Respond with Curiosity (1 minute):** Instead of arguing, ask: "Help me understand what concerns you most about this direction" or "What would need to be true for this to feel right to you?"

4. **Look for Integration:** Seek ways to honor both the change you're proposing and the wisdom contained in the resistance.

This practice transforms resistance from an obstacle to overcome into intelligence to integrate.

Dancing with Resistance: Five Shifts in Change Leadership

From...	To...
Resistance as enemy	Resistance as system intelligence
Heroic effort	Collective capacity
Culture vs. operations	Integrated change
Control-based change	Pattern-based, ecological shifts
Burnout and push	Rhythmic, relational stamina

From Force to Flow: Three Shifts in Empathic System Leadership
- From pushing change to creating rhythm
- From controlling outcomes to tending conditions
- From rescuing people to expanding capacity

11.5 Adaptive Capacity and Sustainable Resilience

From Heroic Leadership to Stewardship

After two years leading culture change at Meridian, Maya found herself at a crossroads. There were genuine signs of transformation: several departments had developed thriving collaborative cultures, patient experience scores were improving in tandem with operational metrics, and a cadre of advocates throughout the organization were championing the integrated approach. Yet the work remained unfinished. Some departments persisted in old patterns, certain leaders continued to frame efficiency and humanity as competing priorities, and institutional inertia continued to exert its gravitational pull toward established ways of operating.

Maya felt torn between pride in what had been accomplished and frustration at how much remained unchanged. Some days she wondered whether the effort was worth it and whether the system's resistance would ultimately prove stronger than her capacity to persist. She had seen other change agents before her burn out, become cynical, or gradually accommodate to the status quo. How could she sustain her commitment for the long journey ahead?

This dilemma highlights perhaps the most personal dimension of systemic resistance: its capacity to exhaust those seeking to create change. The conventional narrative around organizational change often centers on the heroic leader, the visionary individual who drives transformation through sheer force of will and charisma. This framing creates unrealistic expectations and unsustainable pressures on those leading change efforts.

As leadership scholar Peter Senge observes, "The myth of the heroic CEO or the heroic change agent has done enormous damage. It promises what cannot be delivered and sets up those with good intentions for failure and disappointment."

Meaningful change in complex systems cannot be driven by individuals alone, no matter how capable or committed. These patterns reflect not personal weakness, but the inherent limitations of the heroic paradigm itself.

Building Strategic Stamina

A more sustainable approach recognizes that resilience, like change itself, is fundamentally relational. No individual can maintain sufficient resilience in isolation to transform complex systems. As theologian Frederick Buechner observed, "You can't be a light bearer if you're not connected to the power source."

This recognition shifts focus from individual stamina to collective capacity. Networks of relationship and meaning help sustain change agents through difficulty. Regular gathering with others engaged in similar work provides not just practical support, but a crucial sense of normality when change efforts encounter resistance. Connection to transcendent purpose and practice provides perspective and renewal amid challenge. Physical practices that restore energy and presence counter the disembodiment that often accompanies organizational life.

Behind this collective understanding lies a deeper insight: effective change agents work simultaneously with inner and outer systems. They recognize that transformation happens not just in organizational structures and processes but in consciousness itself—the ways of seeing, being, and relating that shape organizational reality.

Resilience as Collective Practice

Beyond psychological considerations lie strategic dimensions of resilience, particularly around pacing and patience. Ronald Heifetz encourages leaders to "get on the balcony" and create a capacity to maintain perspective on longer-term patterns while engaged in immediate challenges. This perspective allows them to distinguish between temporary setbacks and fundamental obstacles, adjusting strategy accordingly.

This strategic resilience involves the ability to work with longer time horizons than typical organizational planning cycles, recognizing that meaningful cultural shifts often require years rather than quarters. It includes skill in identifying and celebrating incremental progress rather than focusing exclusively on the gap between current reality and ultimate vision.

For Maya at Meridian, building strategic resilience involved creating a "council of allies" across departments, maintaining a progress journal, and working with an external coach. Perhaps most importantly, she reframed her role from heroic transformer to steward—someone who cares for something without controlling it (Block, 2008). This shift allowed her to remain committed to Meridian's transformation, while releasing the unrealistic expectation that she alone was responsible for its full realization.

11.6 Dancing with the System

Co-Creating Change That Endures

Three years into her culture change work, Maya was meeting with a newly formed advisory council composed of representatives from across Meridian: clinical staff, administrators, and support services. They were reflecting on what had been learned through the ongoing transformation process.

"I remember how this started," said James, a veteran physician. "You came with this beautiful vision of a more human-centered culture. We all nodded and smiled, but honestly, most of us were thinking 'here we go again, another initiative that will fade away when it hits reality.' And we weren't entirely wrong."

Maya nodded, appreciating his candor.

"But what's been different," James continued, "is how you responded when things didn't go as planned. Instead of pushing harder or blaming us for not getting it, you got curious. You asked why. You listened to what wasn't working. And then, this is the key part, you adjusted based on what you heard."

Other council members nodded in agreement. Teresa, a nurse manager, added: "It feels less like you're trying to impose a new culture and more like we're discovering together what Meridian can become, honoring what's valuable in our history while evolving where we need to change."

This exchange captures a crucial reframing: from struggling against systems to dancing with them. As systems scientist Donella Meadows observed, "We can't control systems or figure them out. But we can dance with them!" This dance involves neither domination nor surrender, but rather an engaged partnership that respects the system's intelligence while steadily inviting it toward greater wholeness.

From Resistance to Co-Creation

Throughout this chapter, we have challenged conventional wisdom about organizational resistance. Rather than viewing it as an obstacle to overcome, we have explored resistance as a teacher that reveals system dynamics, a guardian that protects essential functions, and a partner in co-creating more sustainable change.

This reframing suggests a fundamental shift in orientation:

- From seeing resistance as obstruction to recognizing it as intelligence about the system that can inform more integrated change efforts
- From treating efficiency and humanity as competing values to understanding them as mutually reinforcing dimensions of organizational effectiveness
- From fighting against institutional inertia to working with systemic realities through coordinated, multi-dimensional intervention
- From exhausting ourselves through heroic effort to building collective resilience and strategic stamina for the long journey of transformation

The path forward requires abandoning several comforting illusions: the myth of the heroic leader who single-handedly transforms organizations; the false dichotomy between efficiency and humanity that forces unnecessary tradeoffs; the naive belief that good intentions and compelling visions can overcome institutional inertia without structural support; and the unsustainable pattern of exhausting change agents in service of unrealistic expectations.

In their place emerges a more mature approach to organizational transformation, one that works with rather than against systemic realities. This approach recognizes that meaningful change emerges through persistent, intelligent engagement over time; that efficiency and humanity reinforce rather than oppose each other; that institutional inertia contains both wisdom and limitation; and that sustainable change requires collective rather than merely individual resilience.

For Maya at Meridian, this mature understanding led to "collaborative evolution," a process where change emerged through ongoing dialogue between change agents and the system itself. Rather than adhering rigidly to predetermined plans, she created regular forums where implementation challenges could surface, be examined collectively, and inform adjustments. Rather than treating resistance as opposition to be overcome, she invited it into the conversation as valuable intelligence about what the organization truly needed.

The result wasn't a perfect realization of her initial vision. But it was something potentially more valuable: an authentic expression of what Meridian could become when human values and operational realities were integrated rather than opposed. The organization didn't transform overnight, but it evolved steadily toward greater humanity without sacrificing—indeed, while enhancing—its effectiveness in delivering care.

The invitation is not to fight harder against resistant systems but to engage them more wisely, with greater awareness of their complex dynamics, deeper respect for their embedded intelligence, and more sustainable strategies for gradual yet fundamental transformation. This dance with resistance becomes not an obstacle to change but the very path through which more human, more meaningful, and ultimately more effective organizations emerge.

When we learn to dance with resistance rather than fight it, something remarkable happens: the system begins to teach us how it wants to evolve. The resistance becomes our partner in creating change that honors both what the organization has been and what it might become.

This dance with resistance prepares the ground for the cultural transformation we'll explore in the next chapter. If empathy at the system level begins with sensing, it culminates in shaping through rituals, rhythms, and regenerative design. Culture is not what resists change; it is what holds it.

Chapter 12

Culture as Container

"The fish is the last to discover water."

—Chinese proverb

Empathy doesn't lead culture—culture makes empathy possible. It's the invisible architecture that either amplifies or inhibits our shared capacity to care.

For too long, we've treated culture like furniture—something static that surrounds the "real" work. But culture isn't background; it's the nervous system. It's the living container that determines what can be felt, expressed, and ultimately known within any human system.

The Cultural Container Framework

Every organizational culture can be understood through two essential dimensions: **psychological safety** (the belief that you won't be punished for speaking up) and **courageous challenge** (the willingness to engage productively with discomfort). Together, they define four cultural containers:

	Low Challenge	High Challenge
High Safety	**Comfort Trap**: Pleasant but stagnant	**Regenerative Container**: Growth through connection
Low Safety	**Disengaged Culture**: Neither safe nor growing	**Threat Culture**: High pressure, low trust

Most organizations unconsciously default to comfort traps or threat cultures. The regenerative container—high safety and high challenge—creates conditions where empathy, innovation, and authentic connection naturally emerge.

The Day the Culture Changed

Eastbrook Medical Center had always prided itself on efficiency. The 320-bed hospital consistently ranked in the top quartile for operational metrics, with physician productivity, bed turnover rates, and cost containment that made it the envy of regional competitors. But beneath these impressive statistics lurked troubling realities: staff burnout rates were climbing, medical errors had increased 12% over two years, and interdepartmental collaboration was deteriorating.

The shift began unexpectedly during a routine Tuesday morning leadership meeting. Dr. Sarah Chen, a respected neurologist and newly appointed Chief Medical Officer, was presenting a case review of a near-miss incident when she did something unprecedented in Eastbrook's leadership culture. Instead of the standard clinical analysis focused on process failures, she paused, took a deep breath, and said, "I need to acknowledge that I contributed to this situation. When the nurse called with concerns, I was dismissive. I was tired, rushing between patients, and I missed important signals that should have altered my assessment."

The room fell silent. In Eastbrook's unspoken but powerful cultural code, leaders didn't publicly acknowledge their mistakes. They

211

certainly didn't reveal vulnerability. And they absolutely never admitted to dismissing a nurse's input. For a moment, the cultural container seemed to wobble precariously. Would Dr. Chen be subtly ostracized, her credibility diminished?

Then the CEO, James Anderson, who had led Eastbrook for eleven years, leaned forward. "Thank you, Sarah," he said. "That couldn't have been easy to share. It makes me wonder how many times I've done something similar without recognizing it." He paused. "In fact, I realize our entire approach to these reviews suggests we believe perfect performance is possible in an imperfect system. That's not just unrealistic. It's creating the very conditions that make errors more likely."

Within days, something shifted in Eastbrook's cultural atmosphere. Physicians began acknowledging uncertainty more openly. Nurses reported feeling more comfortable raising concerns. Cross-departmental meetings that had been tense and territorial became more collaborative. Nothing in the organizational chart had changed. No new policies had been implemented. No restructuring had occurred. Yet somehow, the unwritten rules governing behavior had been fundamentally altered.

Eastbrook's transformation illustrates a profound truth: organizational culture functions as a container that shapes what can be felt, expressed, and ultimately known within a human system. This living container simultaneously holds us together and shapes what we're able to become together.

By container, we mean the relational, emotional, and symbolic conditions that regulate what is safe, visible, and possible within a system.

Against the dominant narrative of culture as a tool for performance, we will explore culture as a collective nervous system that regulates our capacity for connection, creativity, and meaning-making. We will examine how rituals and rhythms create the boundaries of this container, how some cultures extract empathic energy while others regenerate it, and how we might measure what truly matters beyond narrow performance metrics.

The most profound invitation of this chapter is to recognize that we never merely work "in" a culture. We are the culture, participating in its living emergence. The container shapes us, but we are also the container.

12.1 Culture Creates Possibility

Culture operates below conscious awareness, regulating our collective nervous system like an invisible conductor orchestrating a symphony.

To understand what happened at Eastbrook Medical Center, we need to see beyond the visible behaviors to the invisible regulatory patterns beneath. Dr. Chen's vulnerable disclosure and CEO Anderson's supportive response didn't merely model new behaviors. They recalibrated the organization's collective nervous system, changing what felt safe to express, what could be acknowledged, and ultimately what could be addressed together.

Most culture change efforts fail because they target the wrong layer of human experience. They focus on what people think rather than how they feel. They attempt to engineer beliefs rather than cultivate conditions. They treat culture as a machine to be built rather than a garden to be tended.

Culture as condition means recognizing that empathy, innovation, collaboration, and learning don't happen despite organizational context. They happen because of it. The cultural container either enables these capacities or constrains them. Change the container, and behaviors shift organically. Ignore the container, and even the most well-intentioned initiatives will be absorbed by existing patterns.

Consider Westfield Financial, a mid-sized investment firm where leaders prided themselves on creating a "psychologically safe" environment. They held workshops on feedback, encouraged innovation, and publicly celebrated their open culture. Yet when consultant Maya Rodriguez observed team meetings, she noticed a striking pattern: whenever uncertainty arose, bodies tensed, eyes flicked toward the senior executive, and conversation narrowed to technical details rather than exploring broader implications.

When Maya shared this observation, leaders were genuinely surprised. Their espoused values and conscious intentions emphasized openness, but their collective nervous system operated according to different rules. Whenever conversations entered uncertain territory (precisely where the greatest learning potential existed), the organization's regulatory system automatically narrowed perception and response to maintain safety through certainty.

We don't build culture; we inhabit and co-regulate it. The path toward more adaptive cultures begins with this recognition: culture is not something we have, but something we are.

12.2 Culture Regulates Us

Daniel Siegel (2020) observes that the brain is a social organ, made to be in relationship. Our neural architecture develops and functions in constant response to others, creating patterns of resonance that shape all subsequent perception and response. Individual dynamics become exponentially more complex in organizations. The collective nervous system emerges from countless moment-to-moment interactions: subtle facial signals, voice tone shifts, who speaks when, what emotions are mirrored or dampened, which cues trigger activation or withdrawal.

If culture functions as collective nervous system regulation, then leadership fundamentally involves co-regulation: the capacity to influence others' nervous system states through relationship, like tuning forks that cause nearby instruments to resonate. "Culture, as a system of energy and information flow, can be seen as a shared pattern of interaction that shapes the emergence of our mental lives. When these patterns promote integration, they support mental health; when they impair integration, they can lead to chaos or rigidity in our collective systems" (Siegel & Drulis, 2023, p. 7). Recent neuroimaging research demonstrates this isn't metaphorical. Leaders' emotional states can literally synchronize team members' neural patterns within minutes (Boyatzis et al., 2012). Research in polyvagal theory shows that our nervous systems constantly scan for cues of safety and danger in our social environment, with special attention to those with power or authority (Porges, 2011). A leader's physiological state (whether regulated, dysregulated, or disconnected) becomes a powerful regulatory cue for the entire system.

This regulation happens not primarily through what leaders say but through how they embody their role: their tone, posture, facial expressions, attention patterns, and energetic presence. Leaders who maintain regulated presence amid challenge create "islands of safety" where exploration becomes possible. Those who become dysregulated (whether through anxiety, anger, or shutdown) transmit that dysregulation throughout the system, narrowing collective perception and reinforcing defensive responses.

This understanding illuminates what happened at Eastbrook Medical Center. Dr. Chen and CEO Anderson didn't just model vulnerability; they demonstrated regulated responses to uncertainty and error. By maintaining present, connected engagement with difficult realities (neither becoming defensive nor shutting down), they shifted the organization's collective nervous system from threat-orientation to learning-orientation. Their embodied capacity to stay regulated while discussing mistakes provided a crucial signal: we can acknowledge imperfection without losing either safety or competence.

The Founding Imprint

This explains why founding teams exert such profound influence on organizational culture, often decades after their departure. Early patterns of regulation become baseline assumptions about what feels normal. The organization's initial regulatory patterns (how it managed anxiety, distributed attention, processed disagreement, and responded to setbacks) establish neural pathways that become the path of least resistance for all future interactions.

A technology company's founding team worked in wartime conditions during its early years, with brutal hours, intense criticism of imperfection, and regular adrenaline-fueled crisis responses. Twenty years and thousands of employees later, this regulatory pattern persisted despite multiple culture change initiatives. The collective nervous system continued to generate crisis energy even when objective circumstances didn't warrant it. Employees described "always feeling behind" and "never being able to catch your breath" even during objectively successful periods.

The regulatory understanding fundamentally challenges how we approach culture change. The dominant model treats culture as a mechanism to be engineered through structural interventions and behavioral prescriptions. The regulatory understanding suggests something closer to cultivation: creating conditions where the collective nervous system can expand its capacity for awareness, connection, and complexity.

Reflection Question: Where do you observe nervous system regulation happening in your organization? How do you contribute to collective regulation or dysregulation through your presence and embodied responses?

12.3 The Grammar of Rituals

Rituals are the encoded grammar of collective life. They reveal, more than tell, what matters most.

At Globex Technologies, new team members receive their orientation not just in formal onboarding sessions but through the lived experience of the organization's distinctive rhythms. From the daily "morning markets" where teams share quick status updates while standing, to the weekly "triad time" where rotating groups of three discuss challenges across functional boundaries, to the quarterly "perspective days" where external speakers broaden the organization's thinking, these consistent patterns create what anthropologists would recognize as ritual.

These rhythms derive their power not from their productivity value, though they certainly contribute to performance. Their deeper function lies in what they communicate implicitly about what matters, how we relate, and who belongs. The standing updates convey that brevity and energy are valued. The cross-functional triads signal that boundary-spanning is expected. The perspective days demonstrate that outside viewpoints aren't threats but resources.

The most powerful rituals are often the mundane, repeated practices that structure daily work: how meetings begin and end, how decisions get made, how conflicts are addressed, how successes and failures are processed. Cultural strength emerges not from slogans but from these repeated, embodied patterns that shape what feels safe, valued, and expected without needing to be stated (Schein & Schein, 2017).

The Invisible Signals

These everyday rituals function as channel factors: small but consequential patterns that direct energy along particular pathways, like the banks of a river shaping water flow. The ritual of beginning team meetings with operational updates versus personal check-ins creates entirely different pathways for subsequent conversation. The practice of having executives present finished strategies versus involving multiple levels in strategy formation shapes not just those specific decisions but the organization's entire relationship with authority and expertise.

What makes these patterns ritualistic rather than merely routine is their symbolic dimension: the implicit messages they carry about what matters, who belongs, and how we relate. Unlike values statements that operate cognitively, rituals engage our bodies, emotions, and relationships simultaneously.

Ritualization establishes a privileged contrast, differentiating itself from other ways of acting (Bell, 1992). Through ritualized action, abstract values become concrete experience.

A financial services organization discovered this distinction when attempting to shift from transactional to relationship-based client service. Their initial approach emphasized cognitive understanding through training and communication. The transformation accelerated dramatically when they introduced ritual changes: client meetings began with relationship-building before transaction discussion, team gatherings included reflection on client impact rather than just financial results, and performance reviews incorporated client relationship quality equally with revenue metrics.

12.4 The Pulse of Rhythms

Rhythms establish the temporal dimensions of the cultural container, profoundly influencing what's possible within it.

Beyond specific rituals lie the broader rhythms that structure organizational life: the patterns of gathering and dispersing, focusing and reflecting, pushing and recovering. The dominant rhythm in most contemporary organizations remains acceleration: the compression of ever more activity into finite time. This accelerative rhythm privileges immediate response over reflective consideration, quantity over depth, and activity over impact.

It creates a regulatory environment where the nervous system remains perpetually activated. Perception narrows to the urgent at the expense of the important.

The countercultural act in such environments is rhythm diversity: like the changing tides in an ecosystem, deliberately cultivating different temporal qualities. A professional services firm discovered the power of rhythmic intervention when addressing burnout and innovation challenges. Rather than adding wellness programs to an unchanged temporal structure, they fundamentally redesigned their rhythmic container: introducing "low tide" periods for reflection, quarterly "pause weeks" for renewal, and meeting-free focus days for deeper work.

These changes weren't merely about work-life balance but about creating a container where different modes of thinking and being became possible. The slower rhythms enabled reflective, integrative mental processes that allow for breakthrough insight rather than merely reactive response (Kahneman, 2011).

You can feel when a team is losing trust before anyone says it aloud. That's culture at work: not in a poster, but in a glance, a silence, a skipped meeting.

PRACTICE: THE CULTURAL RHYTHM AUDIT

Gather your team for 30 minutes and explore these questions together:

1. **What are our recurring rituals?** Identify the formal and informal practices that structure your collective experience. Which send signals of inclusion? Which might inadvertently exclude?
2. **Which rhythms energize us? Which deplete us?** Notice the temporal patterns that either build or drain collective energy. Are there times when everyone feels chronically overwhelmed or consistently creative?
3. **What "unsaid" rules shape behavior here?** Name the implicit expectations that everyone knows but nobody discusses. What happens when these rules are broken?
4. **When do we feel collectively regulated versus reactive?** Identify situations where your team maintains calm, connected presence versus situations that trigger collective stress responses.

The power of this practice lies not in perfect answers but in making the invisible patterns visible together. Simply naming these elements creates the possibility of consciously evolving them.

12.5 When Culture Drains or Restores Us

Not all empathic cultures are created equal. Some extract our caring capacity; others restore it.

Six months after Dr. Chen's pivotal disclosure, Eastbrook Medical Center was showing measurable changes: patient safety indicators had improved 18%, interdepartmental collaboration scores had risen, and staff retention was trending upward. But perhaps the most significant shift was subtler: staff reported feeling less emotionally depleted at the end of their shifts, even though the work itself remained demanding.

This points to a crucial distinction between cultures that extract empathic energy and those that replenish it. The conventional approach to building empathic cultures often focuses on encouraging more caring, more emotional availability, more interpersonal connection. While these intentions are noble, they can inadvertently create "emotional labor overload": organizational expectations that deplete rather than sustain human capacity for care.

Creating the Regenerative Container

The heart of sustainable empathic culture lies in achieving the regenerative container shown in our framework: the dynamic balance of psychological safety and courageous challenge that creates conditions for both connection and growth.

Google's "Project Aristotle" identified psychological safety as the single most important factor differentiating high-performing teams (Duhigg, 2016). Yet safety without challenge creates comfort zones rather than growth environments. True safety enables challenge rather than eliminating it (Edmondson & Lei, 2014).

The conventional understanding of psychological safety often conflates it with comfort or pleasantness, leading to cultures that prioritize harmony over honesty. A more accurate understanding recognizes psychological safety not as the absence of challenge, but as the container condition that makes productive engagement with challenge possible (Edmondson, 2018).

A technology company discovered this when addressing product quality issues. Initial attempts at creating "safe" feedback sessions resulted in vague conversations that preserved harmony while avoiding technical challenges. The breakthrough came when leaders established new container conditions: technical disagreements would be engaged directly but depersonalized; curious questions would be valued above definitive assertions; and learning would be prioritized over blame.

At Eastbrook Medical Center, Dr. Chen's disclosure demonstrated the integration of safety and courage. Her acknowledgment of error represented genuine courage, made possible by a container where she sensed it would be safe enough to take that risk. CEO Anderson's response then reinforced and expanded that container, making similar expressions of vulnerability safer for others.

Diagnosing Your Cultural Container
Questions for reflection:
- Do people in your organization feel safe admitting mistakes and uncertainties?
- Are difficult truths spoken, or do they remain in hallway conversations?
- When conflicts arise, does your team engage directly or retreat to politeness?
- Do you notice energy building or draining during team interactions?

Your answers reveal whether you're operating in a regenerative container or one of the other three quadrants in our framework.

12.6 Tending the Container

We don't measure the health of a garden by counting its flowers. We sense the vitality of the soil, the quality of light, the rhythm of the seasons.

Twelve months into Eastbrook Medical Center's cultural transformation, the board requested a comprehensive assessment of progress. The leadership team gathered rich data: improved patient safety metrics, reduced staff turnover, enhanced collaboration scores. Yet something felt incomplete about these measurements. "These numbers tell us things are improving," observed Dr. Chen, "but they don't quite capture what's actually changed in how it feels to work here."

This observation highlights a fundamental challenge in organizational life: our measurement systems often focus on performance outcomes while missing the container conditions that make those outcomes possible. We track what organizations produce but not how they function as human systems.

Beyond Downstream Metrics

The conventional measurement approach focuses overwhelmingly on downstream metrics: lagging indicators that measure outputs after they've occurred. While these outcome measures matter, they suffer from fundamental limitations. If the goals of a system are defined in terms of outputs, the outputs will be produced at the expense of undesirable impacts elsewhere (Meadows, 2008).

At Eastbrook Medical Center, leaders developed a complementary measurement system they called "container health indicators":

Safety-Courage Balance: Regular pulse surveys measuring both psychological safety ("I feel safe admitting mistakes") and courageous challenge ("I feel encouraged to challenge ideas") on simple 1-5 scales.

Error Processing Capacity: Rather than just tracking error rates, they measured how errors were addressed through brief post-incident surveys asking "How was this handled?" with learning-focused versus blame-focused response options.

Boundary Permeability: They tracked cross-departmental collaboration through simple questions like "How easily can you get input from other teams when needed?"

Rhythm Diversity: Monthly check-ins on energy levels and the balance between high-intensity and reflective time.

These measures revealed patterns invisible to conventional metrics. Departments with the highest psychological safety scores also demonstrated the most productive engagement with challenging quality issues. Units with greater rhythm diversity maintained higher sustained productivity than those with constant high-pressure activation.

Measurement as Sense-Making

Perhaps the most profound shift in measurement involves recognizing that metrics themselves don't create meaning. People do. Numbers provide data, but only human interpretation transforms that data into meaningful insight (Weick, 1995).

Eastbrook embodied this principle through quarterly "sense-making forums" where diverse stakeholders (clinical staff, administrators, patients, community members) gathered to interpret performance data together. Rather than executives analyzing metrics in isolation, these forums created shared meaning through dialogue across perspectives.

Just as culture is not something we have but something we are, so too must measurement become something we interpret, not merely calculate. We shape the container, and the container shapes what we value enough to measure.

12.7 Culture Changes One Leader at a Time

"Leaders lead through the stories they tell." —Howard Gardner

The most profound culture shifts happen not in boardrooms or town halls, but in the quiet moments between two people. A manager helping a direct report see a new possibility. A coach teaching someone how to have a difficult conversation with dignity. A senior leader making the hard decision to part ways with someone whose behavior undermines the values, no matter how talented they might be.

This is the relational reality that frameworks often miss: culture changes one person at a time, through the patient work of individual relationships. Howard Gardner's research on leadership reveals that effective leaders don't just communicate vision through grand gestures; they lead through the stories they tell in countless small moments (Gardner, 1995). "In one-on-one settings, the leader can adapt the story to the specific needs and experiences of the individual, creating a sense of personal connection and trust. This relational approach is particularly effective in changing minds, as it allows the leader to address individual concerns and co-create a narrative that aligns with the follower's identity" (Gardner, 2004, p. 108).

The Coaching Moment That Shifted Everything

At Eastbrook Medical Center, one of the most significant culture shifts didn't happen during Dr. Chen's public disclosure, but in a private conversation weeks later. A department head named Marcus had been struggling with how to address a nurse who consistently dismissed patient concerns. Traditional approaches had focused on policy compliance and documentation. But in a coaching session with Dr. Chen, the conversation took a different direction.

"Marcus," Dr. Chen said, "I'm curious about your experience with Sarah. When you watch her interact with patients, what do you notice in your own body?"

Marcus paused. "I get tense. I find myself wanting to intervene, but I don't know how without seeming like I'm micromanaging."

"That tension you feel might be exactly what patients are experiencing," Dr. Chen reflected. "What if we thought about this not as a policy issue, but as helping Sarah reconnect with why she became a nurse in the first place?"

This conversation led Marcus to approach Sarah completely differently. Instead of citing protocols, he asked about her experience with difficult patients. Instead of focusing on compliance, he explored what made her feel most effective as a caregiver. The result wasn't immediate compliance, but a genuine shift in how Sarah understood her role. More importantly, it changed how Marcus approached coaching conversations with his entire team.

This story illustrates what research on behavior change confirms: sustainable transformation happens through relationship, not mandate. Albert Bandura's work on social learning theory demonstrates that people change behavior primarily through modeling and social reinforcement, not through abstract principles (Bandura, 1977). The most powerful culture shifts occur when trusted leaders help individuals see new possibilities for themselves.

The Voices That Emerge

Culture change isn't about converting everyone. It's about empowering the people who care to speak up, model better behavior, and gradually shift what feels normal. As more people experience these individual coaching moments, their voices begin to emerge to counteract less positive influences.

At Eastbrook, this became visible in unexpected ways. Nurses began speaking up more quickly when they had concerns. Physicians started asking for input before making decisions that affected other departments. The number of "crucial conversations" (Patterson, Grenny, McMillan, & Switzler, 2012) increased dramatically, not because people were taught a technique, but because they had experienced what it felt like to be truly heard and supported in difficult moments.

Research on positive deviance in organizational change supports this pattern. Rather than trying to fix everyone, the most effective culture interventions identify and amplify the people who are already embodying desired behaviors, allowing their influence to spread naturally through the system (Pascale, Sternin, & Sternin, 2010).

The Patient Work of Cultural Leadership

This relational approach requires a different kind of stamina from leaders. It's the patient work of:

- **Having the same conversation multiple times** until new patterns stick

- **Modeling vulnerability** in your own coaching relationships
- **Making tough decisions** about who stays and who goes, based on behavior not just performance
- **Catching people** doing things right and helping them understand the impact
- **Creating safe spaces** for individual reflection and growth

The research on coaching effectiveness reveals why this individual approach works. A meta-analysis by Theeboom, Beersma, and van

Vianen (2014) found that individual coaching produces measurable improvements not just in individual performance, but in team dynamics and organizational culture. The ripple effects of one well-coached leader can transform an entire department.

The Story-Shaping Conversations

Every coaching conversation is an opportunity to shape the stories people tell themselves about leadership, about their capabilities, and about what's possible in their organization. These aren't abstract narratives but lived experiences that become part of someone's identity as a leader.

Consider these coaching questions that reshape internal narratives:

- "What would it look like if this team felt as supported as you felt in our conversation today?"
- "When you think about the leader who most influenced your development, what did they do that you could adapt for your style?"
- "If your team could solve this challenge without you having to fix it, what would need to be true?"

These questions don't provide answers; they invite leaders to author new stories about their role and their team's potential.

The Accumulating Effect

Culture becomes the accumulated effect of these countless individual moments of care, courage, and consistency. Each coaching conversation, each thoughtful decision about performance issues, each time a leader chooses vulnerability over defensiveness contributes to the emerging story of "how we do things here."

This understanding reframes culture work from system engineering to relationship building. The container framework provides useful concepts, but the real work happens in the space between two people, where trust is built and new possibilities are explored. Culture changes not through initiatives but through the gradual transformation of how leaders relate to their people, one conversation at a time.

12.8 Culture as the Amplifier of Collective Einfühlung

Einfühlung—"feeling into"—is not just a personal trait. It is a **relational and systemic intelligence** that arises when conditions allow groups to sense into what's real, what's emerging, and what matters most.

Culture determines whether this capacity for collective sensing can flourish—or whether it is shut down.

In **threat cultures** (high challenge, low safety), individual nervous systems stay activated. Perception narrows. People scan for danger rather than truth. *Einfühlung* contracts into self-protection, and the group loses its capacity to feel into complexity.

In **comfort trap cultures** (high safety, low challenge), surface harmony masks deeper tensions. People "feel into" what is pleasant or expected—but not what is true. The group's empathic acuity dulls through underuse.

In **regenerative containers** (high safety, high challenge), the nervous system is regulated and present. People can "feel into" both individual experience and system dynamics. *Einfühlung* becomes **collective wisdom**—a shared ability to sense what wants to happen.

In these cultures, **empathy becomes a form of perception**—not merely interpersonal, but deeply systemic.

Culture, then, is not just a regulatory system. It is a sensing organ.

Dr. Chen's moment at Eastbrook catalyzed transformation not through policy, but through the sudden expansion of *Einfühlung*. Everyone in the room felt the shift. And that shared feeling—a collective attunement to truth, vulnerability, and possibility—reshaped what the organization could become.

The Insight

We are not merely building better cultures.

We are cultivating **the conditions for shared empathic intelligence**—for *Einfühlung* to emerge as a system-wide capacity.

Leadership in such systems is no longer about directing behavior from above. It is about **tending the nervous system of the whole,** cultivating the conditions where *Einfühlung* becomes our collective way of knowing.

Conclusion: The Living Container

As Eastbrook Medical Center continued its evolution, leaders recognized that transformation wasn't a one-time event but an ongoing journey of individual relationships and collective emergence. The container had been transformed through countless one-on-one conversations, coaching moments, and decisions about who belonged and who didn't.

Rather than engineering culture through top-down interventions, they learned to cultivate it through conscious participation in its emergence. We can't direct a living system, but we can influence it through the quality of our relationships and the stories we tell about what's possible (Wheatley, 2006).

Throughout this chapter, we have explored culture as a living container that simultaneously holds us together and creates conditions for emergence. We've seen how this container functions as a collective nervous system, how rituals and rhythms give it form, and how the balance of safety and courage determines whether cultures drain or restore our empathic capacity.

But perhaps most importantly, we've recognized that culture changes through the patient, relational work of individual leadership. Every coaching conversation, every moment of vulnerability, every thoughtful decision about performance and belonging contributes to the emerging story of "how we do things here."

The invitation is to recognize culture not as something we engineer from outside but as the living medium we collectively create through countless individual moments of care, courage, and consistency. We are always participating in culture's continuous emergence, one relationship at a time.

Culture whispers what is possible—and we respond, not by writing new rules, but by learning to listen.

Simple Steps for Container Cultivation

Start with One Conversation: Choose one person you coach or lead. In your next one-on-one, ask: "What would make you feel most supported in your leadership right now?"

Notice Your Stories: Pay attention to the narratives you tell in coaching moments. Are you helping people see new possibilities for themselves and their teams?

Practice Patience: Cultural shifts happen through the accumulation of individual transformations. Celebrate when someone has a breakthrough in how they see their role.

Stay Consistent: Culture emerges from what you actually do in difficult moments. Each coaching decision either reinforces or undermines the culture you're cultivating.

Cultural Container Assessment

Use this framework to audit your organization's unspoken messages about empathy and belonging.

Cultural Signal	What It Reveals	Positive Indicators	Warning Signs
Meeting Beginnings	Emotional tone setting	Personal check-ins, space for connection	Immediate task focus, no relationship time
Error Response	Safety for vulnerability	Learning questions, curiosity	Blame, defensiveness, cover-ups
Decision Process	Inclusion vs. hierarchy	Multiple voices heard, input sought	Single decider, limited consultation
Conflict Handling	Trust in difficult conversations	Direct engagement, curiosity	Avoidance, behind-closed-doors complaints
Time Allocation	What matters most	Reflection time protected	Constant action, no pause
Recognition Patterns	What gets valued	Collaboration celebrated	Only individual achievement rewarded
Information Flow	Transparency and trust	Open sharing, accessible data	Need-to-know basis, information hoarding
Physical/Virtual Spaces	Belonging signals	Inclusive design, equal access	Status symbols, exclusionary setup

Reflection Questions:

- Which signals in your organization currently support empathic connection?
- Where do you notice gaps between stated values and experienced reality?
- What one signal could you influence to better support psychological safety and courageous challenge?

Chapter 13
DESIGNING WHAT MATTERS

What the World Forgets, You Remember

"The only thing of real importance that leaders
do is to create and manage culture."
— **Edgar H. Schein**

You don't need more tools. You need less noise.

Einfühlung isn't something you perform—it's something you remember. Something you practice. It lives in the space between stimulus and story—before the explanation, before the strategy, before the speech.

In a world obsessed with optimization, measurement, and visibility, you chose something else: to feel.

To feel into what others ignore. To stay in contact with what systems forget. To sense before knowing, to imagine beyond precedent, to respond without hardening, and to replenish what effort erodes.

You didn't arrive here for a fix. You came for a return.

Reclaiming the Rhythm

Throughout this book, we've explored a different kind of intelligence. One that doesn't show up on performance reviews or dashboards. One that doesn't reward you for looking busy, but for staying awake. Awake to nuance. Awake to contradiction. Awake to what stirs.

The Human Engine is not a model you master. It's a rhythm you remember.

Feel what others filter out. Discern what's emerging. Imagine what's not yet visible. Respond with clarity, not compliance. Replenish before the system depletes it all.

It's not linear. It's not static. And it's not for everyone.

But it is for you.

Because somewhere along the way, you noticed. Maybe a twitch. Maybe a fracture. Maybe a dissonance that wouldn't go away.

And instead of numbing out, you leaned in.

We started this journey with a simple recognition: that something was missing from how we understand empathy in organizational life. We were told empathy was about being nice, about agreeing, about making people comfortable. We discovered it was actually about staying present with complexity, about sensing what's really happening beneath the surface, about having the courage to respond to what we feel even when systems resist.

Your sensitivity wasn't a liability but an intelligence. Your ability to feel into systems wasn't emotional overwhelm but sophisticated sensing. Your discomfort with mechanical approaches to human complexity wasn't weakness but wisdom.

What You Discovered

In this exploration of Einfühlung, profound truths emerged:

Presence is not passive but fiercely active. It takes tremendous energy to stay awake when systems are designed to put you to sleep. To keep sensing when everything around you rewards reactivity. To maintain contact with your deeper knowing when the world insists on surface solutions.

Without boundaries, empathy dissolves into absorption. Feeling into others' experience doesn't mean taking it on. You can sense deeply without losing yourself. Discernment is not judgment, but the capacity to hold complexity without collapsing into simplicity.

Imagination is not fantasy but moral vision. The ability to sense what wants to emerge is not naive optimism but pragmatic hope. Envisioning different possibilities is not escaping current reality but engaging it more fully.

Response is not reaction. The space between what happens and how you engage is where wisdom lives. You can act from clarity rather than urgency, from understanding rather than assumption, from care rather than control.

Sustainable empathy requires rhythm. You cannot pour from an empty cup. Caring for others begins with tending to your own capacity. Replenishment is not selfish but essential infrastructure for continued service.

What the Organization Taught You

Through Maya's journey at Meridian Healthcare, the culture transformations at Eastbrook Medical Center, and countless other examples, you witnessed how organizations either cultivate or constrain our capacity for connection:

Culture functions as a collective nervous system that either supports our ability to stay present with each other or triggers us into defensive reactivity. The unspoken rules and rhythms of organizational life shape what we can feel, express, and ultimately address together. When culture becomes a sensing organ, Einfühlung can emerge as collective intelligence.

Resistance often reveals what the system most needs to face. What appears as obstruction often points toward essential truths that change efforts have overlooked. Learning to sense what resistance is protecting leads to more sustainable transformation.

When systems lack empathy, suffering isn't accidental—it's designed. Wellness programs and empathy training cannot compensate for structures that fragment attention, compress time, and reward efficiency over connection. The most caring people often burn out fastest in systems that extract empathy without replenishing it.

Power dynamics shape empathic capacity. Hierarchical structures can limit empathy to flowing upward while those with less formal power are expected to attune constantly to those above them. Redistributing voice and influence creates conditions where mutual empathy becomes possible.

What You Remember

But beneath all the frameworks and practices, beneath the organizational insights and systemic understanding, you remember something more fundamental:

You remember what it feels like to be truly seen. Those moments when someone stayed present with your complexity rather than rushing to fix or change you. When your perspective was received not as a problem to solve, but as wisdom to integrate.

You remember what it feels like to see truly. Those instances when you sensed beyond someone's words to what they were really trying to communicate. When you felt their struggle or hope or confusion and could respond from that deeper understanding.

You remember what it feels like when systems support rather than constrain empathy. Those rare organizational experiences where you could bring your full capacity for care to your work. Where sensing was valued alongside strategy, where taking time to understand was seen as essential rather than inefficient.

You remember that this is possible. Not just in isolated moments but as a way of being. Not just individually but collectively. Not just in special circumstances but in the ordinary complexity of daily organizational life.

You Are the Signal

Empathy isn't dead. But what we've called empathy? That's done.

The performative caring that prioritizes looking compassionate over being present. The emotional labor that demands endless giving without support for renewal. The surface listening that hears words but misses meaning. The conflict avoidance that mistakes harmony for connection.

There's nothing wrong with performing care. The problem arises when the performance replaces presence—when looking empathetic becomes more important than actually being with someone.

You are not here to revive emotional performance or performative care. You are here to lead with contact. To live in rhythm. To bring coherence where control has taken root.

In systems that reward speed, you practice patience. In cultures that demand certainty, you stay present with questions. In environments that fragment attention, you maintain sustained focus on what matters most.

You are the quiet pattern breaking through. You are the signal in the noise.

The Practices You Carry

As you return to the complexity of your organizational life, you carry with you not just concepts but embodied practices:

The practice of presence that begins each day with sensing rather than immediately doing. That creates space between meetings for transition and integration. That approaches every interaction with curiosity about what's really happening beneath the surface.

The practice of discernment that can hold multiple truths without rushing to resolution. That discerns what's urgent from what's essential, what's reactive from what's wise, between individual needs and collective wisdom.

The practice of moral imagination that can sense possibilities beyond current constraints. That envisions not just what is but what could be. That holds hope as a discipline rather than a feeling.

The practice of skillful response that acts from understanding rather than assumption. That engages conflict as an invitation to deeper connection, rather than a problem to avoid. That speaks truth in ways that can be heard.

The practice of sustainable caring that tends to your own capacity as carefully as you tend to others'. That recognizes replenishment as essential infrastructure for service rather than selfish indulgence.

What You Change Simply by Being

Perhaps most importantly, you carry the understanding that your presence itself is intervention. The quality of attention you bring to any situation can shift its possibilities. Modeling a different way of being gives others permission to access their own capacity for deeper engagement.

When you stay present in a meeting where everyone else is distracted, you create an island of focus that others can join. When you respond to conflict with curiosity rather than defensiveness, you demonstrate that disagreement can lead to understanding. When you acknowledge your own mistakes and limitations, you make it safer for others to bring their full humanity to work.

You don't need to fix every broken system or heal every organizational wound. You simply stay in contact with what matters—and respond from there.

Tomorrow morning, when you walk into your office, attend that video call, or sit in that challenging meeting, you'll have a choice. You can join the frenetic pace of reactivity, or you can bring the quality of presence that shifts everything. You can listen for what people are trying to say beneath their words. You can sense what the system is really needing. You can respond from wisdom rather than urgency.

This is how transformation happens: one moment of Einfühlung at a time.

The Spiral Path

This book doesn't end with a call to action. It ends with a deeper contact.

A spiral. A return.

The spiral is not a circle—it is movement with memory. Each return is also a progression. You are not back where you began. You carry wisdom now. You lead from resonance.

You were always this sensitive. You were always this aware. You were always capable of this depth of connection and care. What you've gained through this exploration is not empathy itself but permission to trust what you've always known.

Permission to value sensing alongside strategy. Permission to move at the speed of trust rather than the speed of transaction. Permission to honor complexity rather than demanding simplicity. Permission to care sustainably rather than depleting yourself in service to others.

The world will continue to reward different things. Systems will still resist the very intelligence they most need. Cultures will still prioritize efficiency over connection, productivity over presence, compliance over care.

At Eastbrook, the culture still isn't perfect. But people now pause before meetings to breathe. Nurses ask questions they once held back. Marcus coaches his team differently. The signal remains fragile—but it's there. And it's growing.

But you will remember.

You will remember that beneath every organizational challenge is a human complexity that deserves attention. That behind every resistance is an intelligence that wants to be heard. That within every system is a possibility for greater coherence and care.

You will remember that empathy is not soft sentiment but sharp intelligence. Not individual skill but collective capacity. Not nice-to-have, but essential infrastructure for any human system that wants to thrive rather than merely survive.

You were never too much. You were always the thread connecting what was fragmented, sensing what was hidden, imagining what was possible, responding to what was needed, sustaining what wanted to emerge.

The Capacities You Embody
Now you carry forward not just practices but embodied truths:

You sense not just to understand—but to stay present. You discern not just to choose—but to honor tension. You imagine not to escape—but to reveal what wants to be. You respond not to solve—but to serve. You replenish not as retreat—but as restoration of your sacred engine.

These are not skills to master, but rhythms to live. Not techniques to apply, but ways to be fully present with the complexity of human experience.

And when this capacity is nurtured in teams, cultures, and systems—it becomes more than personal practice. It becomes collective sensing. A way entire organizations begin to feel again. The individual rhythm catalyzes systemic transformation, one relationship at a time.

The Question That Remains

As you close this book and return to your organizational life, one question remains:

What will you feel into today that others are filtering out?

What conversation needs your presence? What tension contains intelligence that's waiting to be heard? What possibility is trying to emerge that needs your attention? What response is yours to give? What part of your capacity needs tending so you can continue this work?

The world needs people who can sense beyond the obvious, who can discern wisdom within complexity, who can imagine possibilities beyond current constraints, who can respond from clarity rather than reactivity, who can sustain their caring over time rather than burning out in service to others.

The world needs you to remember what it forgets: that we are human beings having a shared experience, and that the quality of attention we bring to that experience shapes everything that becomes possible.

You have everything you need. You always did.

Now trust what you feel. And begin.

Einfühlung: the capacity to feel into shared experience. Not to take it on, but to touch it. Not to fix it, but to sense it. Not to control it, but to be present with it.

This is your intelligence. This is your gift. This is your work.

The feeling revolution begins with you.

Begin again. Gently. Fiercely. Fully.

The world is waiting for what only you can feel.

Epilogue
THE THREAD WE FOLLOWED

We began with a quiet ache—hard to name, but deeply felt. Not a problem to solve, but a signal to listen to. A subtle tension in the system. A sense that something essential was thinning.

Through this journey, we didn't just define empathy. We walked with it. We let it unsettle us—expand us, disrupt us, deepen us.

We came to see empathy not as a soft skill or a leadership trait, but as a movement—a living force threading through our capacity to sense, discern, imagine, respond, and replenish.

And in doing so, we reframed something even more fundamental: What it means to be human. Not an optimized unit. Not a disembodied mind. But a complex, creative, vulnerable being— wired for rhythm, connection, and renewal.

The Human Engine isn't a solution. It's an invitation. To lead differently. To design more wisely. To return, again and again, to what matters most.

And though we may not always name it outright, we have been tracing something else along the way—resilience. Not the kind that grits its teeth and pushes through, but the kind that breathes, mends, and dares to begin again.

So wherever you are—in your work, your system, your season—

Pause. Listen. There's a thread still pulling you forward.

Follow it. It will take you somewhere true. Again.

Appendix A
THE HUMAN ENGINE PRACTICE GUIDE

Turning Insight into Capacity

You've traveled far—through ache, through action, through design. Now comes the real work: turning insight into capacity.

This guide is your invitation to take what you've learned and live it forward.

Empathy is not a trait you have or don't. It is a rhythm you live into. In a world that often reduces empathy to emotional labor or technique, the Human Engine offers something different: a regenerative model of empathy in motion.

This is not a checklist. It's not a formula. It's a rhythm—a way of working and being that honors complexity, connection, and care.

> *FIVE CAPACITIES FOR EMBODIED LEADERSHIP*
> *FEEL • DISCERN • IMAGINE • RESPOND • REPLENISH*

Each capacity is a practice in motion, a form of empathy with a particular posture, purpose, and possibility. These five interwoven capacities form a relational system—you may enter anywhere, but they move together. You don't need to master all five. You simply need to begin—wherever you feel the pull.

How to Use This Guide

Whether you're leading a team, shaping a system, or rethinking how you show up, this guide offers a way to start. Each capacity includes:

- **What This Builds** – the inner strength and outer signal of this practice
- **Key Signals** – how to know it's time to lean in
- **Practices to Try** – small, everyday ways to embody this capacity
- **Reflection Prompts** – questions to unlock clarity, alone or with others
- **When It Matters Most** – moments when this capacity becomes critical

Start Here: Choose Your Entry Point

- **Feeling overwhelmed or rushing past nuance?** ⇢ Start with **FEEL**
- **Stuck in indecision or avoiding difficult truths?** ⇢ Start with **DISCERN**
- **Energy feels flat or ideas feel recycled?** ⇢ Start with **IMAGINE**
- **Know what to do but not doing it?** ⇢ Start with **RESPOND**
- **Running on empty or exhausted?** ⇢ Start with **REPLENISH**

FEEL – Attuning to What the Body Knows

What This Builds: Interoceptive awareness. Presence. The ability to attune before reacting.

FEEL is where empathy begins—noticing subtle internal and relational cues before emotion or analysis kicks in. This is the body's first signal that something matters.

Key Signals

You're rushing past nuance. Tension is in the air but unnamed. Your gut knows something your mouth won't say. You're overriding early signals in the name of productivity or politeness.

Practices to Try

Personal Level:

- **90-Second Scan:** Pause and scan your body head to toe. Notice where there's tension or openness
- **Sensory Anchor:** In moments of pressure, focus attention on one anchor (breath, feet, hands)
- Set 3 daily reminders to check in with what your body is telling you

Team Level:

- Start meetings with 60 seconds of silence to arrive fully
- **Check-in Ritual:** Begin decision-making by naming what your body is sensing
- Ask "What's the energy in the room?" before diving into agenda items

System Level:

- Include "emotional weather reports" in regular organizational check-ins
- Design spaces that support different somatic needs
- Train leaders to recognize and respond to collective felt sense

Reflection Prompts

- What have I sensed in my body lately but dismissed?
- What sensations reliably accompany clarity—or confusion?

- What is this moment asking me to feel?

When It Matters Most

In high-stakes meetings. Before big decisions. When your team feels unsettled. During organizational change.

When This Is Missing: Burnout disguised as productivity. Conflicts that seem to come from nowhere. Decisions made in emotional blindness.

DISCERN – Choosing Wisely When Values Collide

What This Builds: Boundaries. Values alignment. Clarity in complexity.

DISCERN is empathy's ethical core—it helps us hold multiple truths without collapsing into binary choices. It doesn't avoid tension, it stewards it.

Key Signals

You're stuck between conflicting needs. You're saying yes to too much. You're avoiding truth to preserve harmony. You're mistaking agreement for empathy.

Practices to Try

Personal Level:
- **Two Truths Practice:** Name two conflicting truths and sit with both. Don't rush resolution
- **Ethical Pause:** Ask, "Who benefits from this choice? Who might be harmed?"
- Map values in conflict: Draw columns listing what each choice honors vs. what it costs

Team Level:

- Name explicitly who benefits and who's left out of proposed solutions
- Create decision frameworks that include impact on relationships, not just outcomes
- Practice distinguishing between urgent and important together

System Level:

- Embed values-based decision criteria into formal processes
- Create feedback loops that surface unintended consequences quickly
- Design systems that make ethical considerations visible, not optional

Reflection Prompts

- When have I mistaken agreement for empathy?
- What truths am I avoiding because they create tension?
- How do I honor truth without harming trust?

When It Matters Most

In ethical dilemmas. When setting priorities. When navigating organizational power. During resource allocation.

When This Is Missing: Overwhelm disguised as caring. Resentment from overcommitment. Values compromised in the name of harmony.

IMAGINE – Seeing Beyond What Is Present

What This Builds: Creative vision. Strategic possibility. Moral imagination.

IMAGINE is empathy projected forward—moral vision in motion. It helps us move beyond reaction into possibility, envisioning futures rooted in empathy, not just efficiency.

Key Signals

Energy is low. Ideas feel recycled. People are solving the same problems with no breakthrough. Urgency has shrunk your imagination.

Practices to Try

Personal Level:

- **Vision Shift:** Ask, "If we honored what we're sensing, what would become possible?"
- **Futures Sketching:** Describe your work at its most alive—not efficient, but alive
- Share one "impossible" idea each month

Team Level:

- Create "future stories" sessions where you imagine successful outcomes in detail
- **Third Way Exercise:** When caught between either/or, ask: "What's the creative third way?"
- Hold quarterly "possibility mapping" conversations

System Level:

- Designate formal time and space for non-pragmatic thinking
- Create innovation processes that include emotional and relational outcomes
- Celebrate experiments that fail but expand thinking

Reflection Prompts

- Where have I let urgency shrink my imagination?
- What futures are waiting beneath the discomfort I'm avoiding?
- What becomes possible if we lead with connection?

When It Matters Most

During reinvention. When burnout becomes cynicism. When strategy needs soul. In long-term planning.

When This Is Missing: Cynicism masquerading as realism. Innovation that lacks human consideration. Solutions that address symptoms but not root causes.

RESPOND – Translating Insight into Action

What This Builds: Courageous follow-through. Credibility. Alignment between values and behavior.

RESPOND is where empathy becomes real—moving from knowing to doing. It doesn't require perfect plans, just action from presence.

Key Signals

You're avoiding a hard conversation. The right thing is known, but not done. Action is happening, but it feels hollow. You're playing small despite knowing better.

Practices to Try

Personal Level:

- **Micro-Move:** Take one concrete step—the hard email, honest question, overdue pause
- **Integrity Map:** Write down the action that most aligns with your values, not your comfort zone

- Say the thing you're avoiding—kindly. Start with "I've been hesitant to mention this, and..."

Team Level:
- Create "integrity check-ins" where teams assess alignment between values and actions
- Practice difficult conversations as skill-building, not crisis management
- Close loops by following up on decisions and commitments

System Level:
- Design accountability systems that support growth, not punishment
- Create clear pathways for surfacing and addressing misalignment
- Measure integrity indicators alongside performance metrics

Reflection Prompts
- What am I avoiding acting on, even though I feel the need?
- What's the cost of silence, delay, or playing small?
- What action would align me with what I already know?

When It Matters Most
When people are watching. When culture is shaped by silence. When inaction feels like betrayal. During crisis moments.

When This Is Missing: Good intentions without follow-through. Teams that know what's right but don't act. Trust eroded by inconsistency.

REPLENISH – Restoring What Has Been Spent

What This Builds: Sustainable energy. Long-term resilience. A culture of humanity.

REPLENISH is not retreat—it's rhythm. It's how we honor the body as infrastructure so empathy can continue.

Key Signals

You're exhausted but pushing through. Rest feels like a luxury. People are burning out or numbing out. Empathy has shifted from energizing to exhausting.

Practices to Try

Personal Level:

- **Recovery Ritual:** End hard meetings with a somatic reset—shake out, walk, silence
- **Boundary Audit:** List three boundaries that would help preserve your energy
- Identify what truly restores you (not numbs you) but actually returns you to yourself

Team Level:

- Embed brief restoration moments into long meetings
- Create team rituals for recovery after intense periods
- Name and address emotional residue from difficult conversations

System Level:

- Design sustainable rhythms into organizational processes
- Measure and reward sustainable performance, not just peak performance

- Create cultural permission for restoration without guilt

Reflection Prompts
- When do I notice empathy shifting from energizing to exhausting?
- What restores me—truly?
- How do I signal to others that rest is allowed?

When It Matters Most
After intensity. Amid transition. During cultural renewal. When planning long-term initiatives.

When This Is Missing: Burnout normalized as dedication. Leaders who can't model sustainability. Innovation stifled by exhaustion.

Living the Cycle

The Human Engine is not a technique. It's a cycle. A rhythm. A way of leading—and a way of living.

You start where you are. You feel what's real. You discern what matters. You imagine what could be. You respond with integrity. You return to restore. And then—you begin again.

This is empathy in motion. This is how leadership becomes a living practice. This is how systems begin to heal.

A Daily Practice

Morning (2 minutes)
- **FEEL:** What am I sensing in my body as I begin this day?
- **DISCERN:** What matters most today?

- **IMAGINE:** What's one possibility I want to explore?

Evening (3 minutes)
- **RESPOND:** What did I follow through on? What did I avoid?
- **REPLENISH:** What does my body/mind/spirit need right now?

Team Workshop Outline

Opening (15 min): Introduce the five capacities and the cycle **Practice Round (30 min):** Work through a current team challenge using all five capacities **Individual Reflection (10 min):** Which capacity does each person most need to develop? **Collective Commitment (15 min):** What's one way to embed this rhythm into how we work together? **Closing (10 min):** Name one insight and one commitment

The Practice of Becoming

You don't have to master it all. You only have to begin. The Human Engine doesn't give you answers—it restores your ability to stay with what matters long enough for the right questions to surface.

You don't manage this model. You listen to it. You live it. Not as a toolkit. As a rhythm.

Trust the ache. Follow the cycle. And build what matters.

"The heart that breaks open can contain the whole universe." — Joanna Macy

Glossary

A

Affective Presence
The state of embodied, non-performative attention that allows others to feel seen, heard, and held. It is not technique, but attunement.

Architectures of Detachment
The often-invisible systems, workflows, and norms designed—intentionally or not—to suppress emotional engagement in favor of control, speed, or comfort. A central critique of performative empathy cultures.

Autonomic States
The physiological modes—ventral vagal, sympathetic, and dorsal vagal—that shape our capacity to connect, empathize, or shut down in response to our environment.

B

Body as Instrument
The notion that the leader's body is not just a vessel for the mind, but a tool for sensing relational, ethical, and systemic information in real time.

C

Collective Intelligence
The emergent wisdom of a group, amplified when empathic sensing, psychological safety, and co-regulation are present.

Compassionate Response
Empathic action rooted in presence and clarity rather than distress or overwhelm. Distinguished from empathic distress by its generative, sustainable nature.

Conflict Repair
The act of restoring relationship and resonance after tension or misalignment, often through acknowledgment, accountability, and presence.

Co-regulation
The shared neurobiological process through which nervous systems stabilize one another in real time. Essential for collective intelligence, relational safety, and the flow of systemic empathy.

Cultural Performances of Care
Superficial displays of empathy used to signal concern without disrupting systemic power dynamics or emotional risk.

Curiosity Loop
A state of open inquiry activated by subtle signals, discomfort, or unspoken tension. An essential precursor to empathic imagination.

D

Dadirri
An Indigenous Australian concept of "deep listening" or inner stillness, often cited in contrast to Western notions of projection-based empathy.

Discernment
The capacity to navigate ambiguity, tension, and competing truths without collapsing into binary choices. A core function in the Human Engine.

Disconnection Creep
The slow normalization of emotional detachment, often justified by performance metrics or efficiency.

Dorsal Vagal State
A freeze or shutdown mode in the nervous system, often associated with numbness, collapse, or social withdrawal.

Dynamic Empathy
Empathy as a living, adaptive process. It evolves with context, relationship, and nervous system state—not a static trait, but an expressive, embodied rhythm.

E

Einfühlung
German for "feeling into." The original, embodied concept of empathy rooted in aesthetics, ethics, and perception—not projection or performance.

Empathic Distress
A reactive state in which witnessing suffering leads to emotional overwhelm, avoidance, or burnout rather than action.

Empathic Infrastructure
The physical, procedural, and cultural design of an organization that enables (or disables) its collective capacity to sense, respond, and care at scale.

Empathic Signal
A somatic cue—flutter, tightness, heat—that reflects attunement to another's unspoken emotional or relational state.

Embodied Intelligence
The knowledge carried in and through the body—felt before it is thought, essential to empathy, ethics, and leadership.

Ethical Signal
A bodily alert that arises in the presence of moral dissonance or conflict—e.g., a gut sense that something is wrong.

F

Feel
The Human Engine's foundational capacity: to register, through the body, what matters before it can be named or explained.

Fragile System
An organization or culture where truth is filtered, dissent is punished, and sensing is unsafe or impossible.

H

Holding Environment
A relational or organizational space that contains complexity, discomfort, and ambiguity without collapsing. Enables adaptive growth and transformation.

Human Engine (The)
The central model of this book. A regenerative cycle of five empathic capacities—Feel, Discern, Imagine, Respond, Replenish—that sustain connection, creativity, and complexity-responsiveness in systems and leadership.

I

Imagine
The capacity to envision alternative futures, possibilities, and outcomes—not fantasy, but empathic foresight in service of transformation.

Inclusive Attention
Deliberate attentional practices that ensure all signals—especially from marginalized or quieter voices—are heard and integrated.

Interoception
The inner sense of bodily awareness (e.g., heartbeat, breath, gut feeling), foundational to emotional clarity and empathic accuracy.

L

Listening Lab
A designed space within an organization for surfacing weak signals, emotional truths, or subtle misalignments before they escalate.

N

Nervous System Hospitality
Creating environments that support regulation, rest, and responsiveness rather than reactivity. A prerequisite for systemic empathy.

P

Performance Trap
The habitual substitution of scripted empathy for actual presence. Empathy as theater rather than truth.

Polyvagal Theory
A framework explaining how safety, connection, or threat states in the nervous system impact empathic capacity.

Presence vs. Performance
A foundational distinction. Presence is authentic, embodied, and responsive. Performance mimics empathy through scripted behaviors without risking vulnerability or transformation.

R

Reactivity Culture
A high-pressure norm that suppresses reflection, amplifies urgency, and disables subtle sensing.

Regulator of Resonance
A person—often informal—whose nervous system stabilizes group dynamics and fosters collective sensing.

Relational Field
The energetic and emotional space between people where meaning, mood, and memory are exchanged and shaped.

Replenish
The often-overlooked capacity of the Human Engine. Replenishment counters burnout and empathic depletion by restoring nervous system regulation and emotional vitality.

Resonant System
A team or culture tuned to internal and external signals. Able to sense and respond without losing alignment.

Restorative Attention
Deliberate focus on what soothes and restores the nervous system. Necessary for leadership stamina and empathic depth.

S

Safe Enough to Feel
The threshold of physiological and emotional safety needed to permit full empathic engagement.

Sense
A synonym for Feel. Highlights the role of embodied perception in noticing what systems or stories conceal.

Signal Fatigue
The depletion caused by chronically ignoring or overriding empathic cues. A pathway to numbness or burnout.

Signal Journal
A practice for tracking bodily cues throughout the day, strengthening signal literacy and interoceptive awareness.

Signal Literacy
The refined capacity to detect, interpret, and act on subtle bodily, emotional, or systemic cues. It turns intuition into intelligence and transforms reaction into wisdom.

Somatic Intelligence
Knowing that arises from and through the body—not as metaphor, but as literal data.

Sovereign Empathy
Empathy that honors boundaries. It stands with another without collapsing into them.

Strategic Numbness
The adaptive suppression of empathy to function under stress or achieve goals—effective in the short term, costly in the long term.

Structural Signal Suppression
The systemic silencing of discomfort, difference, or dissent—often through hierarchy, fear, or polite avoidance.

Systemic Empathy
Empathy that lives not in individuals alone, but in the structures, feedback loops, and values of an organization. It's designed, not just felt.

T

Tuning
The micro-adjustment of presence, posture, or pace in response to unspoken cues. A leadership practice of sensing and syncing without losing self.

U

Unfelt Cost
The hidden toll of performative culture—disconnection, depletion, and lost potential that never makes it onto the balance sheet.

V

Ventral Vagal State
The physiological state of calm social engagement. The optimal zone for empathy, presence, and collective intelligence.

Venturing into Vulnerability
Choosing to sense, speak, or stay present in emotionally risky spaces. A foundational act of empathic leadership.

W

Weak Signal
A subtle early cue of change, misalignment, or truth. Often dismissed—but essential to foresight and innovation.

Wholeness
The integration of intellect, emotion, sensation, and spirit in leadership. A return to undivided selfhood.

Window of Tolerance
The neurobiological range within which a person can function effectively without being overwhelmed or shut down.

Wisdom of Discomfort
The insight that emerges when we remain present with what disturbs us. Discomfort is not failure—it's information.

Witnessing
Being fully present with another's truth without needing to fix, solve, or retreat. A quiet act of profound care.

REFERENCES

Ackoff, R. L. (1994). The democratic corporation: A radical prescription for recreating corporate America and rediscovering success. Oxford University Press.

Ahmed, S. (2010). The promise of happiness. Duke University Press.

Amabile, T. M. (1996). Creativity in Context. Westview Press.

Arnsten, A. F. T. (2009). Stress signalling pathways that impair prefrontal cortex structure and function. Nature Reviews Neuroscience, 10(6), 410-422.

Ashkanasy, N. M., Härtel, C. E. J., & Daus, C. S. (2002). Diversity and emotion: The new frontiers in organizational behavior research. Journal of Management, 28(3), 307-338.

Badaracco, J. L. (1997). Defining moments: When managers must choose between right and right. Harvard Business School Press.

Balcetis, E., & Dunning, D. (2006). See what you want to see: Motivational influences on visual perception. Journal of Personality and Social Psychology, 91(4), 612-625.

Bandura, A. (1977). Social learning theory. Prentice Hall.

Bandura, A. (1997). Self-efficacy: The exercise of control. W.H. Freeman.

Barsade, S. G. (2002). The ripple effect: Emotional contagion and its influence on group behavior. Administrative Science Quarterly, 47(4), 644-675.

Bateson, G. (1972). Steps to an ecology of mind: Collected essays in anthropology, psychiatry, evolution, and epistemology. University of Chicago Press.

Batson, C. D. (2011). Altruism in humans. Oxford University Press.

Baumeister, R. F., Sparks, E. A., Stillman, T. F., & Vohs, K. D. (2008). Free will in consumer behavior: Self-control, ego depletion, and choice. Journal of Consumer Psychology, 18(1), 4-13.

Bell, C. (1992). Ritual theory, ritual practice. Oxford University Press.

Bell, C. (1997). Ritual: Perspectives and dimensions. Oxford University Press.

Block, P. (2008). Community: The structure of belonging. Berrett-Koehler Publishers.

Bloom, P. (2016). Against empathy: The case for rational compassion. Ecco.

Bonhoeffer, D. (1959). The cost of discipleship. SCM Press.

Bowen, M. (1978). Family therapy in clinical practice. Jason Aronson.

Boyatzis, R. E., Goleman, D., & Rhee, K. S. (2000). Clustering competence in emotional intelligence: Insights from the Emotional Competence Inventory (ECI). In R. Bar-On & J. D. A. Parker (Eds.), The handbook of emotional intelligence: Theory, development, assessment, and application at home, school, and in the workplace (pp. 343–362). Jossey-Bass.

Brown, B. (2018). Dare to lead: Brave work, tough conversations, whole hearts. Random House.

Bruner, J. (1990). Acts of meaning. Harvard University Press.

Buber, M. (1970). I and thou (W. Kaufmann, Trans.). Charles Scribner's Sons. (Original work published 1923)

Buechner, F. (1993). Wishful thinking: A seeker's ABC. HarperOne.

Cameron, K. (2012). Positive leadership: Strategies for extraordinary performance (2nd ed.). Berrett-Koehler Publishers.

Cameron, K. S., Bright, D., & Caza, A. (2004). Exploring the relationships between organizational virtuousness and performance. Organizational Dynamics, 33(4), 384-399.

Cameron, K. S., & Quinn, R. E. (2011). Diagnosing and changing organizational culture: Based on the competing values framework (3rd ed.). Jossey-Bass.

Catalyst. (2021). The power of empathy in times of crisis. https://www.catalyst.org/reports/empathy-workplace-leadership/

Catmull, E., & Wallace, A. (2014). Creativity, Inc.: Overcoming the unseen forces that stand in the way of true inspiration. Random House.

Chopik, W. J., O'Brien, E., & Konrath, S. H. (2017). Differences in empathic concern and perspective taking across 63 countries. Journal of Cross-Cultural Psychology, 48(1), 23-38.

Cooperrider, D. L., & Whitney, D. (1999). Appreciative inquiry. Berrett-Koehler Communications.

Cozolino, L. (2014). The neuroscience of human relationships: Attachment and the developing social brain (2nd ed.). W.W. Norton.

Craig, A. D. (2002). How do you feel? Interoception: The sense of the physiological condition of the body. Nature Reviews Neuroscience, 3(8), 655-666.

Craig, A. D. (2009). How do you feel—now? The anterior insula and human awareness. Nature Reviews Neuroscience, 10(1), 59-70.

Critchley, H. D., & Garfinkel, S. N. (2017). Interoception and emotion. Current Opinion in Psychology, 17, 7-14.

Csikszentmihalyi, M. (1990). Flow: The psychology of optimal experience. Harper & Row.

Damasio, A. (1994). Descartes' error: Emotion, reason, and the human brain. Putnam.

Damasio, A. (2010). Self comes to mind: Constructing the conscious brain. Pantheon Books.

Dana, D. (2018). The polyvagal theory in therapy: Engaging the rhythm of regulation. W.W. Norton & Company.

David, S. (2016). Emotional agility: Get unstuck, embrace change, and thrive in work and life. Avery.

Deci, E. L., & Ryan, R. M. (2000). The "what" and "why" of goal pursuits: Human needs and the self-determination of behavior. Psychological Inquiry, 11(4), 227-268.

Ryan, R. M., & Deci, E. L. (2020). Self-Determination Theory and the facilitation of intrinsic motivation, social development, and well-being. Psychological Inquiry, 31(2), 123–145. https://doi.org/10.1080/1047840X.2020.1755721

Denning, S. (2011). The leader's guide to storytelling: Mastering the art and discipline of business narrative. Jossey-Bass.

Drayton, B. (2010). Tipping the world: The power of collaborative entrepreneurship. Stanford Social Innovation Review, 8(2), 30-35.

Dreyfus, H. L. (1992). What computers still can't do: A critique of artificial reason. MIT Press.

D'Souza, R., & Reich, A. (2023). Empathy, burnout, and turnover intentions: A longitudinal study of workplace culture. Occupational Health Science, 7(3), 421–438. https://doi.org/10.1007/s41542-023-00145-2

Duckworth, A. (2016). Grit: The power of passion and perseverance. Scribner.

Duggan, W. (2007). Strategic intuition: The creative spark in human achievement. Columbia University Press.

Duhigg, C. (2016, February 25). What Google learned from its quest to build the perfect team. The New York Times Magazine. Retrieved from https://www.nytimes.com/2016/02/28/magazine/what-google-learned-from-its-quest-to-build-the-perfect-team.html

Dutton, J. E. (2006). Energize your workplace: How to create and sustain high-quality connections at work. Jossey-Bass.

Edmondson, A. C. (1999). Psychological safety and learning behavior in work teams. Administrative Science Quarterly, 44(2), 350–383.

Edmondson, A. C. (2018). The fearless organization: Creating psychological safety in the workplace for learning, innovation, and growth. John Wiley & Sons.

Edmondson, A. C. (2019). The fearless organization: Creating psychological safety in the workplace for learning, innovation, and growth. John Wiley & Sons.

Edmondson, A. C., & Lei, Z. (2014). Psychological safety and learning behavior in work teams. Administrative Science Quarterly, 59(2), 350-383.

Edmondson, A. C., & Lei, Z. (2014). Psychological safety: The history, renaissance, and future of an interpersonal construct. Annual Review of Organizational Psychology and Organizational Behavior, 1(1), 23–43.

Ernst & Young. (2023). 2023 EY Empathy in Business Survey. https://www.ey.com/en_us/news/2023/03/ey-us-consulting-study-employees-overwhelmingly-expect-empathy-in-the-workplace

Ewing, J. (2017). Faster, higher, farther: The Volkswagen scandal. W.W. Norton & Company.

Figley, C. R. (1995). Compassion fatigue: Coping with secondary traumatic stress disorder in those who treat the traumatized. Brunner/Mazel.

Figley, C. R., & Burnette, C. E. (2024). Compassion fatigue and organizational stress: The role of powerlessness in empathy collapse. Traumatology, 30(1), 45–53. https://doi.org/10.1037/trm0000421

Fletcher, J. K. (1998). Relational practice: A feminist reconstruction of work. Journal of Management Development, 17(4), 302-320.

Frank, A. W. (2010). Letting stories breathe: A socio-narratology. University of Chicago Press.

Frankl, V. E. (1959). Man's search for meaning. Beacon Press.

Freire, P. (1970). Pedagogy of the oppressed. Continuum International Publishing Group.

Galinsky, A. D., Maddux, W. W., Gilin, D., & White, J. B. (2008). Why it pays to get inside the head of your opponent: The differential effects of perspective taking and empathy in negotiations. Journal of Personality and Social Psychology, 95(5), 1048-1062.

Gallese, V., & Goldman, A. (1998). Mirror neurons and the simulation theory of mind-reading. Trends in Cognitive Sciences, 2(12), 493-501.

Gardner, H. (1995). Leading minds: An anatomy of leadership. Basic Books.

Gardner, H. (2004). Changing Minds: The Art and Science of Changing Our Own and Other People's Minds. Boston, MA: Harvard Business School Press, p. 108.

Geertz, C. (1973). The interpretation of cultures: Selected essays. Basic Books.

Gendlin, E. T. (1978). Focusing. Everest House.

Gino, F., & Kouchaki, M. (2022). Why empathy matters for ethics in organizations. Harvard Business Review. https://hbr.org/2022/09/why-empathy-matters-for-ethics-in-organizations

Goleman, D. (1998). Working with emotional intelligence. Bantam Books.

Goleman, D., & Boyatzis, R. (2008). Social intelligence and the biology of leadership. Harvard Business Review, 86(9), 74-81.

Goleman, D., & Boyatzis, R. E. (2017). Emotional intelligence has 12 elements. Which do you need to work on? Harvard

Business Review. https://hbr.org/2017/02/emotional-intelligence-has-12-elements-which-do-you-need-to-work-on

Goodstein, J. D. (2015). Moral courage. In D. J. Mele & J. A. Werhane (Eds.), The Oxford handbook of business ethics (pp. 551-578). Oxford University Press.

Grant, A. (2017). Originals: How non-conformists move the world. Penguin Books.

Greene, J., & Haidt, J. (2002). How (and where) does moral judgment work? Trends in Cognitive Sciences, 6(12), 517-523.

Grossmann, I., et al. (2020). Wisdom in a complex world: A situated account of wise reasoning and its development. Nature Communications, 11(1), 1716.

Gusnard, D. A., & Raichle, M. E. (2001). Searching for a baseline: Functional imaging and the resting human brain. Nature Reviews Neuroscience, 2(10), 685-694.

Hackman, J. R. (2002). Leading teams: Setting the stage for great performances. Harvard Business Press.

Han, S., & Ma, Y. (2015). A cultural neuroscience approach to the biosocial nature of the human brain. Annual Review of Psychology, 66, 355-379.

Hanh, T. N. (2014). No mud, no lotus: The art of transforming suffering. Parallax Press.

Hargadon, A., & Sutton, R. I. (2000). Building an innovation factory. Harvard Business Review, 78(3), 157-166.

Hasson, U. (2010). I can make your brain look like mine. Harvard Business Review, 88(12), 32–33.

Hasson, U., Ghazanfar, A. A., Galantucci, B., Garrod, S., & Keysers, C. (2012). Brain-to-brain coupling: A mechanism for creating and sharing a social world. Trends in Cognitive Sciences, 16(2), 114-121.

Heifetz, R. A. (1994). Leadership without easy answers. Harvard University Press.

Heifetz, R. A., & Linsky, M. (2002). Leadership on the line: Staying alive through the dangers of leading. Harvard Business School Press.

Heifetz, R., Grashow, A., & Linsky, M. (2009). The practice of adaptive leadership: Tools and tactics for changing your organization and the world. Harvard Business Press.

Hills, H. R., & Kitayama, S. (1991). Culture and the self: Implications for cognition, emotion, and motivation. Psychological Review, 98(2), 224-253.

Hochschild, A. R. (1983). The managed heart: Commercialization of human feeling. University of California Press.

Hofstede, G. (2001). Culture's consequences: Comparing values, behaviors, institutions, and organizations across nations (2nd ed.). Sage Publications.

Hofstede, G., Hofstede, G. J., & Minkov, M. (2010). Cultures and organizations: Software of the mind: Intercultural cooperation and its importance for survival (3rd ed.). McGraw-Hill.

Hojat, M., Louis, D. Z., Markham, F. W., Wender, R., Rabinowitz, C., & Gonnella, J. S. (2013). Physicians' empathy and clinical outcomes for diabetic patients. Academic Medicine, 86(3), 359-364.

Holling, C. S. (2001). Understanding the complexity of economic, ecological, and social systems. Ecosystems, 4(5), 390-405.

Hühn, M. P., & Meyer, R. E. (2024). Embodied empathy in organizations: Sensory cues and adaptive decision-making. Frontiers in Psychology, 15, 1289347. https://doi.org/10.3389/fpsyg.2024.1289347

Immordino-Yang, M. H. (2015). Emotions, Learning, and the Brain: Exploring the Educational Implications of Affective Neuroscience. Norton.

Jha, A. P. (2018). Peak mind: Find your focus, own your attention, invest 12 minutes a day. HarperOne.

Johnson, B. (1992). Polarity management: Identifying and managing unsolvable problems. HRD Press.

Kahneman, D. (2011). Thinking, fast and slow. Farrar, Straus and Giroux.

Kaplan, R., & Kaplan, S. (1989). The experience of nature: A psychological perspective. Cambridge University Press.

Kaplan, S. (1995). The restorative benefits of nature: Toward an integrative framework. Journal of Environmental Psychology, 15(3), 169-182.

Kaufman, S. B., & Gregoire, C. (2015). Wired to create: Unraveling the mysteries of the creative mind. TarcherPerigee.

Kegan, R. (1994). In over our heads: The mental demands of modern life. Harvard University Press.

Keltner, D. (2016). The power paradox: How we gain and lose influence. Penguin Press.

Kimmerer, R. W. (2013). Braiding sweetgrass: Indigenous wisdom, scientific knowledge and the teachings of plants. Milkweed Editions.

Kleitman, N. (1963). Sleep and wakefulness. University of Chicago Press.

Kotler, S. (2021). The art of impossible: A peak performance primer. Harper Wave.

Kotter, J. P. (1996). Leading Change. Harvard Business Press.

Kotter, J. P. (2008). A sense of urgency. Harvard Business Press.

Kovach, M. (2021). Indigenous methodologies: Characteristics, conversations, and contexts (2nd ed.). University of Toronto Press.

Kross, E. (2021). Chatter: The voice in our head, why it matters, and how to harness it. Crown.

Ladkin, D. (2021). Leading with the body: Embodied leadership in practice. Leadership, 17(3), 289-307.

Lakoff, G., & Johnson, M. (1999). Philosophy in the flesh: The embodied mind and its challenge to Western thought. Basic Books.

Lear, J. (2006). Radical hope: Ethics in the face of cultural devastation. Harvard University Press.

Lecoq, J. (2000). The moving body: Teaching creative theatre (D. Bradby, Trans.). Methuen.

Levinas, E. (1969). Totality and infinity: An essay on exteriority (A. Lingis, Trans.). Duquesne University Press.

Levinthal, D. A., & Rerup, C. (2022). Adaptive systems and organizational sensemaking: Toward a theory of sensory integration. Academy of Management Review, 47(3), 456–478. https://doi.org/10.5465/amr.2020.0321

Lipps, T. (1903). Einfühlung, innere Nachahmung, und Organempfindungen. Archiv für die gesamte Psychologie, 1, 185-204.

Lipstadt, D. E. (2019). Antisemitism: Here and now. Schocken Books.

Little Bear, L. (2000). Jagged worldviews colliding. In M. Battiste (Ed.), Reclaiming Indigenous voice and vision (pp. 77–85). UBC Press.

Loehr, J., & Schwartz, T. (2003). The power of full engagement: Managing energy, not time, is the key to high performance and personal renewal. Free Press.

Marcario, R. (2017). Patagonia's CEO says conscious leaders need to stand for something. SOCAP Global. https://socapglobal.com/2017/03/patagonias-ceo-rose-marcario-shares-her-best-advice-for-companies-and-mindful-ceos-on-taking-risks-trusting-your-gut-and-driving-social-change/

Martin, J. R., & Abraham, A. (2012). The neuroscience of imagination: Implications for design. Design Studies, 33(2), 129-142.

Martin, R. L. (2009). The opposable mind: Winning through integrative thinking. Harvard Business Press.

Maslach, C. (2017). Finding solutions to the problem of burnout. Consulting Psychology Journal: Practice and Research, 69(2), 143-152.

Maté, G. (2003). When the body says no: The cost of hidden stress. Alfred A. Knopf Canada.

Meadows, D. H. (1999). Leverage points: Places to intervene in a system. The Sustainability Institute.

Meadows, D. H. (2008). Thinking in systems: A primer. Chelsea Green Publishing.

Merleau-Ponty, M. (1945). Phenomenology of perception. Routledge.

Miller, E. K., & Buschman, T. J. (2018). Working memory capacity: Limits on the bandwidth of cognition. Daedalus, 147(1), 77-87.

Morgan, D. S. (2025). Designing in the Dark: How Curious Leaders Navigate Uncertainty, Shape Possibility, and Create Without a Map. Echo Horizon Publishing.

Morgan, D. S. (2024). Generation Innovate: Unleashing the creative revolution of millennials. Echo Horizon Publishing.

Morgan, D. S. (2025). GOALS: The Ultimate Guide to Personal and Team Triumph. Echo Horizon Publishing.

Morgan, D. S. (2024). The Joy of Discontent: A Soulful Guide to Embracing Restlessness, Reframing Creative Unease, and Finding Beauty in the Unfinished. Echo Horizon Publishing.

Nagoski, E., & Nagoski, A. (2019). Burnout: The secret to unlocking the stress cycle. Ballantine Books.

Nakamura, J., & Csikszentmihalyi, M. (2023). Collective flow and empathic attunement in collaborative settings. Journal of Positive Psychology, 18(4), 567–579. https://doi.org/10.1080/17439760.2022.2093842

Newberg, A. B., & Waldman, M. R. (2016). How enlightenment changes your brain: The new science of transformation. Avery.

Newport, C. (2016). Deep work: Rules for focused success in a distracted world. Grand Central Publishing.

Nussbaum, M. C. (2001). Upheavals of thought: The intelligence of emotions. Cambridge University Press.

Ondobaka, S., Kilner, J., & Friston, K. (2019). The role of interoceptive inference in theory of mind. Brain and Cognition, 112, 64-68.

Oshry, B. (2007). Seeing systems: Unlocking the mysteries of organizational life. Berrett-Koehler Publishers.

Page, S. E. (2007). The difference: How the power of diversity creates better groups, firms, schools, and societies. Princeton University Press.

Pascale, R. T., Sternin, J., & Sternin, M. (2010). The power of positive deviance: How unlikely innovators solve the world's toughest problems. Harvard Business Review Press.

Patagonia. (2023). Our mission. https://www.patagonia.com/our-mission/

Patterson, K., Grenny, J., McMillan, R., & Switzler, A. (2012). Crucial conversations: Tools for talking when stakes are high (2nd ed.). McGraw-Hill.

Perel, E. (2006). Mating in captivity: Unlocking erotic intelligence. Harper.

Phillips, K. W. (2014). How diversity works. Scientific American, 311(4), 42-47.

Polanyi, M. (1962). Personal knowledge: Towards a post-critical philosophy. University of Chicago Press.

Polman, P., & Winston, A. (2021). Net positive: How courageous companies thrive by giving more than they take. Harvard Business Review Press.

Porges, S. W. (2011). The polyvagal theory: Neurophysiological foundations of emotions, attachment, communication, and self-regulation. W. W. Norton & Company.

Porges, S. W. (2021). Polyvagal Theory: A biobehavioral journey to sociality. Frontiers in Integrative Neuroscience, 15, 643612. https://doi.org/10.3389/fnint.2021.643612

Quadt, L., Critchley, H. D., & Garfinkel, S. N. (2022). Interoceptive training to improve emotional clarity and reduce empathic distress. Neuroscience & Biobehavioral Reviews, 135, 104573.

Robison, P. (2019). Boeing's 737 Max: The inside story of how the 'safest plane' became the most controversial. Bloomberg Businessweek, December 9.

Ryff, C. D. (2014). Psychological well-being revisited: Advances in the science and practice of eudaimonia. Psychotherapy and Psychosomatics, 83(1), 10-28.

Sawyer, R. K. (2007). Group genius: The creative power of collaboration. Basic Books.

Schacter, D. L., Addis, D. R., & Buckner, R. L. (2007). Remembering the past to imagine the future: The prospective brain. Nature Reviews Neuroscience, 8(9), 657-661.

Scharmer, C. O. (2009). Theory U: Leading from the future as it emerges. Berrett-Koehler Publishers.

Schein, E. H., & Schein, P. A. (2017). Organizational culture and leadership (5th ed.). Wiley.

Schneider, S. L. (2001). In search of realistic optimism: Meaning, knowledge, and warm fuzziness. American Psychologist, 56(3), 250-263.

Senge, P. M. (2006). The fifth discipline: The art & practice of the learning organization (Revised ed.). Currency.

Senge, P. M., Kleiner, A., Roberts, C., Ross, R., Roth, G., & Smith, B. (1999). The dance of change: The challenges to sustaining momentum in learning organizations. Doubleday/Currency.

Shourkaei, H. K., Sezer, O., & Phillips, N. (2023). Examining sustainable supply chain management via a social-symbolic work lens: Lessons from Patagonia. Business Strategy and the Environment, 32(7), 4922–4938. https://doi.org/10.1002/bse.3397

Siegel, D. J. (2010). The mindful brain: Reflection and attunement in the cultivation of well-being. W. W. Norton & Company.

Siegel, D. J. (2010). The mindful therapist: A clinician's guide to mindsight and neural integration. W. W. Norton & Company.

Siegel, D. J. (2012). The developing mind: How relationships and the brain interact to shape who we are (2nd ed.). Guilford Press.

Siegel, D. J. (2020). The Developing Mind: How Relationships and the Brain Interact to Shape Who We Are (3rd ed.). New York, NY: Guilford Press.

Siegel, D. J. (2023). "An interpersonal neurobiology perspective on the mind and mental health: Personal, public, and planetary well-being." Frontiers in Psychiatry, 14, 1008683. https://doi.org/10.3389/fpsyt.2023.1008683

Simpson, L. B. (2017). As We Have Always Done: Indigenous Freedom Through Radical Resistance. University of Minnesota Press.

Singer, T., & Klimecki, O. M. (2014). Empathy and compassion. Current Biology, 24(18), R875-R878.

Slovic, P. (2007). If I look at the mass I will never act: Psychic numbing and genocide. Judgment and Decision Making, 2(2), 79-95.

Smith, J. A., & Lee, K. (2024). Empathy and customer loyalty: The cost of task-oriented cultures. Journal of Business Ethics, 189(2), 245–260. https://doi.org/10.1007/s10551-024-05512-3

Snowden, D. J., & Boone, M. E. (2007). A leader's framework for decision making. Harvard Business Review, 85(11), 68-76.

Spreitzer, G. M., Porath, C. L., & Gibson, C. B. (2012). Toward human sustainability: How to enable more thriving at work. Journal of Management, 38(4), 1125-1150.

Stein, E. (1989). On the problem of empathy (W. Stein, Trans.). ICS Publications. (Original work published 1917)

Stein, E. (1989). On the problem of empathy (3rd ed.). ICS Publications. (Original work published 1917).

Sweller, J. (2011). Cognitive load theory. In J. P. Mestre & B. H. Ross (Eds.), The psychology of learning and motivation: Cognition in education (pp. 37-76). Academic Press.

Taylor, C. (1989). Sources of the self: The making of the modern identity. Harvard University Press.

The Investopedia Team. (2025, January 24). The success of Patagonia's marketing strategy. Investopedia. https://www.investopedia.com/patagonia-marketing-strategy-8623992

Teece, D. J. (2007). Explicating dynamic capabilities: The nature and microfoundations of (sustainable) enterprise performance. Strategic Management Journal, 28(13), 1319-1350.

Tenbrunsel, A. E., & Smith-Crowe, K. (2012). Ethical decision making: Where we've been and where we're going. The Academy of Management Annals, 2, 545-607.

Theeboom, T., Beersma, B., & van Vianen, A. E. M. (2014). Does coaching work? A meta-analysis on the effects of coaching on individual level outcomes in an organizational context. Journal of Positive Psychology, 9(1), 1–18.

Uhl-Bien, M., & Marion, R. (2009). Complexity leadership in bureaucratic forms of organizing: A meso model. The Leadership Quarterly, 20(4), 631-650.

Ungar, M. (2019). Change your world: The science of resilience and the true path to success. Sutherland House.

Unger, R. M. (2019). The knowledge economy. Verso.

Ungunmerr-Baumann, M. R. (2002). Dadirri: Inner deep listening and quiet awareness. Emmaus Productions.

van der Kolk, B. (2014). The body keeps the score: Brain, mind, and body in the healing of trauma. Penguin Books.

van der Kolk, B. (2014). The body keeps the score: Brain, mind, and body in the healing of trauma. Viking.

van der Kolk, B. (2014). The body keeps the score: Brain, mind, and body in the healing of trauma. Viking Books.

Walker, M. P. (2017). Why we sleep: Unlocking the power of sleep and dreams. Scribner.

Walker, M. U. (2007). Moral understandings: A feminist study in ethics (2nd ed.). Oxford University Press.

Wallace, B. A. (2001). Intersubjectivity in Indo-Tibetan Buddhism. Journal of Consciousness Studies, 8(5-7), 209-230.

Warren, E. (2017). Wells Fargo: Account fraud continues. United States Senate Committee on Banking, Housing, and Urban Affairs.

Watkins, M. (2019). Mutual accompaniment and the creation of the commons. Yale University Press.

Weil, S. (2009). Waiting for God (E. Craufurd, Trans.). Harper Perennial Modern Classics. (Original work published 1949).

Weick, K. E. (1979). The social psychology of organizing (2nd ed.). Addison-Wesley.

Weick, K. E. (1995). Sensemaking in organizations. SAGE Publications.

Weick, K. E., & Sutcliffe, K. M. (2015). Managing the unexpected: Sustained performance in a complex world (3rd ed.). Jossey-Bass.

West, C. (2008). Hope on a tightrope: Words and wisdom. SmileyBooks.

Westley, F., Zimmerman, B., & Patton, M. (2006). Getting to maybe: How the world is changed. Random House Canada.

Wheatley, M. J. (2006). Leadership and the new science: Discovering order in a chaotic world (3rd ed.). Berrett-Koehler Publishers.

Wong, P. T. P. (2014). Meaning-centered approach to research and therapy, second wave positive psychology, and the future of humanistic psychology. The Humanistic Psychologist, 45(3), 207-216.

Woolley, A. W., Chabris, C. F., Pentland, A., Hashmi, N., & Malone, T. W. (2010). Evidence for a collective intelligence factor in the performance of human groups. Science, 330(6004), 686-688.

Worline, M. C., & Dutton, J. E. (2017). Awakening compassion at work: The quiet power that elevate people and organizations. Berrett-Koehler Publishers.

Zahavi, D., & Rochat, P. (2015). Empathy ≠ sharing: Perspectives from phenomenology and developmental psychology. Consciousness and Cognition, 36, 543-553.

ABOUT THE AUTHOR

David S. Morgan is a curious mind on a mission to help people and organizations rediscover their capacity for change. An inventor, CEO, and transformation strategist, he's spent more than thirty years exploring how innovation really happens—from factory floors and nonprofit boardrooms to product labs and startup teams.

In *Einfuhlung*, David reveals how empathy becomes the driving force behind authentic leadership, genuine creativity, and meaningful connection. Drawing from neuroscience, lived experience, and deep observation, he offers a framework for staying human in systems that often forget to be.

David is best known for making complex ideas accessible, practical, and human. His work bridges disciplines but stays grounded in one essential truth: that our shared humanity is our greatest untapped advantage.

He lives and works in New Hampshire, where he finds inspiration in nature, conversation, and whatever's stirring just beneath the surface.

Connect with him at: *davidceonh@gmail.com*

Also by David S. Morgan

- **Ten Steps to Innovating Your Nonprofit** — A hands-on guide to unlocking creativity, designing better programs, and driving real change in mission-driven work.

- **Maple and Brick: A Story of Transformation in a Small-Town Factory** *(A Novel)* — Blending fiction with insight, this novel captures the soul of a struggling town, the grit of reinvention, and the quiet power of human-centered leadership.

- **GOALS: The Ultimate Guide to Personal and Team Triumph** — A high-impact playbook for setting meaningful goals, driving team alignment, and making progress that matters.

- **Generation Innovate: Unleashing the Creative Revolution of Millennials and Gen-Z** — An energizing call to action for emerging leaders—and the organizations ready to support their creative potential.

- **AI-Proof Manifesto: The New Rules of Work in the Age of Intelligent Machines** — A bold, contrarian guide to thriving in the era of AI—by cultivating distinctly human superpowers.

- **The Joy of Discontent** — *A soulful guide to embracing restlessness, reframing creative unease, and finding beauty in the unfinished.* A poetic, provocative exploration of how tension, curiosity, and dissatisfaction fuel our deepest growth.

- **Designing in the Dark** — A poetic-practical guide for leaders facing uncertainty. This book explores how curiosity, attentiveness, and adaptive design can help navigate the unknown, reframe complexity, and shape bold new possibilities—without waiting for a map.

* 9 7 9 8 9 9 9 1 2 3 7 7 7 2 *